Should I Follow a Madhab?

GW00481341

By
Shaykh Mufti Saiful Islām

JKN Publications

© Copyright by JKN Publications

First Published in December 2014

ISBN 978-1-909114-11-1

British Library Cataloguing in Publication Data
A catalogue record for this book is available from the British Library.

Publisher's Note:

Every care and attention has been put into the production of this book. If however, you find any errors they are our own, for which we seek Allāh's ﷻ for-
giveness and reader's pardon.

Published by:

JKN Publications
118 Manningham Lane
Bradford
West Yorkshire
BD8 7JF
United Kingdom

t: +44 (0) 1274 308 456 | w: www.jkn.org.uk | e: info@jkn.org.uk

Book Title: Should I Follow a Madhab?

Author: Shaykh Mufti Saiful Islām

"In the Name of Allāh, the Most Beneficent,
the Most Merciful"

Contents

Preface 6

PART ONE: A DISCUSSION ON TAQLEED *by Mufti Abdul Waheed*... 7

1: Introduction.. 8
1.2. Purpose of this Discussion............................ 10
2. Ijtihād and its Qualifications........................... 10
3: What is Taqleed?.. 12
3.1. Types of Taqleed... 14
3.2. Taqleed and Ittiba...................................... 15
4: Classifications of Texts................................... 16
5: Proofs from the Authentic Sources................... 21
5.1 Qur'ān... 22
5.2. Hadeeth.. 24
5.3. The Existence of Taqleed Shakhsi During the Era of the Sahābah ﷺ... 29
6. Evolvement Period of Taqleed......................... 31
6.1. Era of the Sahābah ﷺ.................................. 31
6.2.The Period of the Tābi'een and Tabi Tābi'een and the Emergence of the Four Schools........................ 36
6.3. The Period of Codification and the Scholars' Adherence to One of the Four Imāms................... 38
7. Why did Talqeed Shakhsi Become Necessary?..... 41
8. Why Choose Taqleed of the Four Schools?......... 44

9: The Recognition of the Four Schools Throughout the World... 47

10: The Statements of Scholars on the Necessity of Taqleed Shakhsi.. 48

11: The Principle of Blocking the Means........................... 52

12: Responding to Some Commonly Posed Questions.......... 53

12.1. Is it possible to strictly adhere to Authentic Hadeeth only?.. 53

12.2. Is it possible to follow all four schools simultaneously?.... 59

12.3. The statement of the Imām, "When a Hadeeth is authentic then that is my Madhab," suggests to prefer Hadeeth over the opinion of the Imām.. 60

12.4. Imām Abū Haneefah's ﷺ knowledge in Hadeeth was weak. 65

13. Conclusion... 66

PART TWO: SOME COMMON QUESTIONS REGARDING TAQLEED by Shaykh Mufti Saiful Islām................. 69

What Does Taqleed Mean?... 70

Should we Follow a Particular Madhab in the Matters of Shari'ah Law?.. 72

How are Laws Deduced from the Holy Qur'ān and Sunnah?.. 81

Why do Taqleed of One Imām only and not Four Simultaneously?.. 93

Preface

All praises are due to Allāh ﷻ, the Lord of the Worlds and May His Infinite Blessings and Mercy be showered upon His Final Messenger, Muhammad ﷺ, his pure family and noble Companions until the Last Day.

This book is a beginner's guide towards understanding Taqleed. It contains relevant information for attaining the true understanding of its concept. Evidences from relevant and authentic sources, classifications and evolvement of Taqleed have been discussed in a simplified manner. It aims to explain the importance of Taqleed and why it is necessary to follow one of the four Madhabs (legal schools) in this day and age.

The Ummah is indebted to the invaluable contribution of the four Imāms for their relentless efforts in preserving the traditional understanding of the legal sources and its correct application, as was understood and practiced during the era of the noble Companions ﷺ. Ones understanding of Islamic Law is deficient without resorting to the works of the four legal schools.

I am grateful towards Shaykh Mufti Saiful Islām (may Allāh ﷻ preserve him and prolong his life) for giving me this opportunity to compile a book on such a topic under his supervision. I pray to Allāh ﷻ to grant us sincerity and reap the benefit from this book, Āmeen.

(Mufti) Abdul Waheed
Teacher at Jāmi'ah Khātamun Nabiyyeen
December 2014/Safar 1436

PART ONE:
A Discussion on Taqleed

1: Introduction

Since the emergence of the four legal schools until the present day, there is no traditional scholarly seminar or major Islamic institute in the world that does not teach or follow either one of the four schools of thought. This suggests that the vast majority of the Ummah adhered to one of the four schools.

It was only post eighteenth century that a minority group emerged advocating a ban on Taqleed (i.e. following) of one of the four schools and condemning such people for discarding the Qur'ān and Sunnah. This condemnation is due to the lack of understanding of the reality and status of these schools and its need in today's day and age. This new innovation of condemning Taqleed has gained momentum quite recently in certain parts of the Islamic world, not to forget the West. The reality of the matter is, that retrospectively speaking, one will rarely discover any Islamic seminary or reputable scholar in the world today who does not adhere or affiliate to one of the four schools of thought, hence, making it nearly impossible for anyone to become independent from any of the four legal schools.

It is said that after the demise of the Holy Prophet ﷺ, the Companions ﷺ continued learning from those who were regarded as the most learned amongst them. The subsequent generations, the Tābi'een, collated their reports, Fatāwa and opinions and then transmitted that knowledge to their students. They even issued verdicts based on their opinions. There are numerous reports where a learned Companion was considered the focal reference point of Islamic learning for the local inhabitants, such as Sayyidunā Abdullāh Ibn Abbās ؓ for the people in Makkah, Say-yidunā Abdullāh Ibn Mas'ood ؓ for the people of Kūfa and so on. It was inevitable that the regional people would adhere to their verdicts.

Following one of the four schools is not a recent phenomenon and nor is it detrimental to ones religion. It will be made apparent that the scholars of the past not only converged upon following one of the four Madhāhib (plural of Madhab - legal school), but they also considered it mandatory to follow a Madhab for those who do not possess the tools of Ijtihād so that the Law of Allāh ﷻ does not become an experiment ground.

The format of the discussion will begin by first explaining the meaning of Ijtihād and its conditions, followed by the basic definition of Taqleed, its classifications and textual evidences. Thereafter it will discuss the emergence of the four schools and their recognition throughout the world. Towards the end, it will present the verdicts given by some of the renowned classical scholars about the necessity in adhering to one of the legal schools and then respond to some common objections.

It must be made clear at this point that though Taqleed implies both restricted and unrestricted form, however throughout this discourse I will imply Taqleed in its restricted form, in other words, restricting to one of the four schools of thought, and not all four in general.

1.2. Purpose of this Discussion.

Taqleed or following one of the four legal schools enables one to view the laws of the Qur'ān and Sunnah more clearly. It is an instrument for facilitating the practice of ones Deen in a coherent and systematic way. This discussion therefore aims to prove that following one of the four schools is not an innovative practice as widely claimed by a minority of people. Rather it is an avenue of following the path of the Salafs – pious predecessors and their interpretive model of Shari'ee sources.

2. Ijtihād and its Qualifications

We begin by primarily explaining what Ijtihād is and what its qualifications are. Ijtihād is the process where a Faqeeh (jurist) exerts all his intellectual efforts in arriving to a legal ruling that is not clear-cut in the textual sources, i.e. Qur'ān and Sunnah. A jurist's aim is to disclose the Law of Allāh ﷺ in cases where there is no clear ruling. This is because certain matters are either nowhere to be found in the Qur'ān and Sunnah or if they are found, they are either ambiguous, based upon a word that has multiple meanings (Mushtarak), conflict of evidences and so on, all of which are open to various interpretations. Part of Ijtihād also entails a bibliographical analysis of each transmitter in the chain of a Hadeeth as well as a textual analysis in determining its reliability.

It must be remembered that the Qur'ān and Sunnah contain broad principles with some detailed laws. Worship, belief systems, morals and historical accounts all fall within the sphere of broad principles whilst the detailed laws mainly focus on the Ahkām-Islamic judicial laws. It might sound surprising for some that, only a small percentage, in comparison to the entire edifice of the Sharī'ah, relates to Ahkām-Islamic juridical laws.

Ijtihād only applies in the sphere of Ahkām to remove the ambiguity in a law or to determine the ruling of a new case by searching for a precedented similitude from the Shar'ee sources and applying it to the new case. Once a scholar reaches the status of Ijtihād, he is then known as a Mujtahid. The classical scholars have outlined those disciplines in which a scholar should master in order to qualify as a Mujtahid;

1.   Arabic Linguistics
2.   Arabic Grammar; both syntax and morphology
3.   The science of Usūl-ul-Fiqh and its related terminologies such as Khās, Ām, Sareeh, Kināyah, Haqeeqat and Majāz and so forth.
4.   Those Qur'anic and Hadeeth injunctions that relate to law with its detailed commentary and an in depth study of Fiqh.
5.   The science of the principles of Hadeeth; the ability of analysing the text and biography of each transmitter in the chain, classifications of the transmission reports, Jarh wa Ta'deel (criticism and authentication), reconciliation between conflicting texts and other related terminologies.
6.   An awareness of the diverse opinions and the Ijtihād of the Sahābah ؓ and the scholars of the subsequent generations.
7.   Asbāb un-Nuzool – the contexts behind revelation
8.   The principles of *Naskh* (abrogation).

3: What is Taqleed?

Taqleed means to accept and follow the opinion of a Mujtahid; the one who is proficient in the tools and mechanisms of Ijtihād when inferring rulings from the four sources of the Sharī'ah (the Qur'ān, Sunnah, Ijmā and Qiyās) and has attained spiritual reformation and piety, without demanding evidence from him. It is not viable for a layperson who has no sound knowledge of the detailed rulings of the Sharī'ah, the methodological principles of inferring rulings from the four sources of the Sharī'ah and is unacquainted with the science of the grading system of Hadeeth, to infer rulings independently.

Following the opinion of the Ulamā (Muslim scholars) has always been the Islamic tradition from its inception. The Ulamā of this Ummah have been vested with the responsibility to preserve the traditional learning and the pureness of Islām.

It can be proudly said that the eponym (reputable jurists after whom the school was named) of the four legal schools; namely Imām Abū Haneefah ﷺ, Imām Mālik ﷺ, Imām Shāfi'ee ﷺ and Imām Ahmad Ibn Hanbal ﷺ, have retained the traditional Islām in its purest form because each of their chain of transmitters links back to the noble Companions ﷺ, who were directly tutored by the Messenger of Allāh ﷺ. So following their interpretive model and understanding of the Sharī'ah enables us to practice the religion in its untainted form that is pleasing to Allāh ﷺ and His Messenger ﷺ.

In regards to the issue of evidence, the Sharī'ah has not obliged a

Mujtahid to present detailed evidences and his methodology of deduction to a layperson. Numerous examples can be cited where a Companion of great scholarship issued a verdict on a matter related to Ijtihād without presenting detailed evidences of their methodological deduction. Shaykh Mufti Taqi Uthmāni relates the following incident; Once Sayyidunā Abū Ayyūb al-Ansārī ﷺ was on his way to perform Hajj when suddenly he lost the camels which he brought for sacrificing (in order for him to come out of Ihrām). On the day of sacrifice, he came to Sayyidunā Umar ﷺ enquiring of what to do in this matter. Sayyidunā Umar ﷺ instructed him to do as those who perform Umrah do (i.e. to shave or cut their hair) and you will be out of Ihrām. Thereafter, he should perform Hajj in the following year and make the sacrifice.

Sayyidunā Abū Ayyūb ﷺ did not demand evidence from him because of his reliance on Sayyidunā Umar's ﷺ level of scholarship. This is somewhat similar to how Taqleed is practiced, in that one relies on the expert opinion of a Mujtahid without demanding evidence because of his trust in his scholarly credentials and piety.

(*Legal Status of Following a Madhab* p. 31, *Muwatta Imām Mālik*)

For a layperson to acknowledge and fully appreciate the evidences, he must primarily understand Usūl ul-Fiqh (legal principles), the Furoo (subsidiary cases), the procedural framework of inferring laws, the various scholarly opinions on that particular subject and the principles of reconciliation between conflicting evidences. These domains are not accessible to the laymen, hence, he is to resort to the opinion of an expert, namely a Mujtahid.

To illustrate this with a simple example, a patient suffering from medical illness registers with a local GP (General Practitioner) because of his lack of qualification in medical science and inability to determine the right remedy for himself. A GP who has dedicated a significant number of years studying and training in the medical field under professionals, is able to determine which medicine is more effective for the patient. A layperson with some sense would dare not take the risk of prescribing medicine for himself, knowing very well the severe repercussions and damage it could cause to his health. He thus, relies on an expert opinion, i.e. GP. In a similar light, if a layperson attempts to solve all the detailed Islamic laws by resorting directly to the Qur'ān and Sunnah himself, with no sound knowledge of the detailed Shar'ee rulings and the methodological framework of inferring rulings, he will end up misguided and utterly confused.

3.1. Types of Taqleed

There are two forms of Taqleed; the first is called Taqleed Ām; an unrestricted form of adherence whereby, one chooses to follow a particular scholar or school in one legal issue and then a different scholar or school in another legal issue.

The second is called Taqleed Shakhsi, a restricted form of Taqleed where a person follows a particular scholar (or a school) in all legal matters.

Both forms of Taqleed existed in the early days. However, after the development of the four legal schools, the later scholars converged upon a consensus to follow only one of the four school (as will be discussed later) in order to shun the doors of more diverse opinions and the possibility of following ones desires.

3.2. Taqleed and Ittiba

Advocates of the abandonment of Taqleed generally assert that they do Ittiba as opposed to Taqleed. They argue that Ittiba is following an expert with recognition of the evidence as opposed to Taqleed which implies blind following without knowing the evidence.

This argument is futile and baseless because as was indicated previously, Taqleed does not imply to blindly following anyone. It is merely reliance on the opinion of an expert jurist without seeking evidence from him. An expert jurist is acquainted and well-rooted in the science of inferring legal issues from the Shar'ee sources and the authentications of reports. The layperson entrusts his legal affairs in the hands of the jurist with the awareness that the jurist has supporting evidences for arriving to such a conclusion which the layperson has no knowledge of. Furthermore, one can only attain recognition of the evidence if one is aware of the principles of Ijtihād.

If this is the case then what use is there for Ittiba in the first place? It turns out that if Ittiba implies to following the opinion of a reputable scholar without demanding proof from them because of their level of expertise in that field, then this makes it no different to Taqleed.

4. Classifications of Texts

All proofs and evidences contained in textual sources are not of the same category. Injunctions of commands and prescriptions vary between each other, depending upon their nature. Not every command is clear and simple as working out a basic equation of 2 + 2. There are two major classifications of evidences;

1: Those textual evidences that are categorical and render no other possible interpretation apart from one. For instance, the fundamentals of belief, obligations (like Salāh, Zakāt etc.) and prohibitions such as consumption of wine, fornication etc.

Ijtihād is not required in this category since matters pertaining to this type are clear and categorical, for instance, the command to establish Salāh, give Zakāt and so on. The connotation of the term Salāh is categorical, implying only one single interpretation which is to carry out a specific mode of worship, five times a day. Giving any other interpretation apart from this, would render it invalid and unacceptable.

2: Those textual evidences which are non-categorical. Such texts require extensive research and critical analysis by a specialist in order to arrive to a conclusion which he deems as closer to the truth. This relates to the elaborative discourses of juristic cases. This category allows scope for other possible interpretation since it involves one exerting every intellectual ability. It is inevitable that the conclusion of one Mujtahid will differ from the other, because not every Mujtahid employs the same methodology of inference as the other. Differences of opinions in this category are therefore probable and tolerable.

Below is an overview of non-categorical types of evidences;
1.   Ambiguity in words.
2.   Words having multiple meanings with the impossibility of applying all of them simultaneously.
3.   *Amr* (Imperative) and *Nahi* (prohibited) have various connotations. For instance, imperative commands (*amr*) could imply obligation, recommendation, concession and so on. The Mujtahid needs to determine the nature of that imperative command by analysing the context in which it is mentioned.
4.   Two conflicting Hadeeth which require the Mujtahid to resort to the principles of resolving conflicting proofs.
5.   No clear ruling of a legal matter is found in the textual sources, so the Mujtahid exerts all efforts in searching for a precedented ruling from the textual sources that are similar to the contemporary one. Once he identifies the similarity, he will then transfer the precedented ruling to the contemporary one. However, the deductive method of one Mujtahid may be different from the other, resulting in both of them reaching to a different conclusion.

Some examples of the second category have been presented below;

EXAMPLE 1:
Allāh ﷻ states in the Holy Qur'ān;

"O Believers! When you stand for Salāh then wash your faces, your hands up to your elbows, masah over your heads and (wash) your feet up to the ankles." (5:6)

The term 'waw' used in this verse is commonly translated as 'and' in English but it has various connotations in the Arabic language; one being sequential (*Tarteeb*) and the other unrestricted plurality (*Mutlaq Jam'a*). The two great Imāms; Imām Abū Haneefah 🕮 and Imām Shāfi'ee 🕮 have differed regarding the functional role of the 'waw' used in this context.

Imām Shāfi'ee 🕮 interprets the 'waw' to be a *Tarteeb* function. In other words, Allāh 🕮 is saying "Wash your faces then your hands then masah....etc." Based on this interpretation, Imām Shāfi'ee 🕮 considers the order and sequence in Wudhu as Fardh.

According to Imām Abū Haneefah 🕮, the function of the term 'waw' in this context implies unrestricted plurality. In other words, no sequence of priority is intended in this verse but instead, it is instructing the believers to wash the limbs and perform masah over their heads regardless of the sequence it is done. Thus, maintaining the order in Wudhu according to Imām Abū Haneefah 🕮 is a Sunnah, not Fardh.

The above two interpretations of the term 'waw' have subsequently led both Imāms to differ in the subsidiary matters. For instance, if someone reversed the method of Wudhu then will the Wudhu still be valid? According to the interpretation of Imām Shāfi'ee 🕮 the Wudhu becomes invalid because maintaining sequence in Wudhu is Fardh. However, according to Imām Abū Haneefah 🕮, Wudhu will still remain valid though one will not attain the full reward of following the Sunnah.

EXAMPLE 2:

In relation to the timings of Salāh, the Messenger of Allāh ﷺ described the expiry of Maghrib time to be the disappearance of the Shafaq. However, Shafaq implies two meanings; the first meaning implies the disappearance of the redness in the sky and the second meaning implies disappearance of both the redness and the whiteness that follows it (i.e. when the horizon becomes completely dark).

Imām Shāfi'ee ﷺ and others have adopted the first meaning, the disappearance of the redness in the sky. However, Imām Abū Haneefah ﷺ has preferred the latter meaning, that is, the disappearance of both the redness and the whiteness.

The subsequent differences that follows from this are for instance, if a person performs his Ishā Salāh whilst there is whiteness effect in the horizon would his Salāh be valid? According to Imām Shāfi'ee ﷺ his Salāh will be valid because Maghrib time has expired. However, Imām Abū Haneefah ﷺ opines that his Salāh will not be valid because Maghrib time has not yet expired.

EXAMPLE 3:

An example of two conflicting evidences, both of which are equally authentic, is the issue of marrying during the state of Ihrām. All of the Imāms unanimously agree that to consummate during the state of Ihrām is prohibited and violates the sanctity of Ihrām. However, is it permissible to just have the Nikah performed in the state of Ihrām?

Imām Shāfi'ee 🌸 views that it is not permissible to marry whilst in the state of Ihrām. This is based upon the Hadeeth reported by Imām Muslim 🌸 in his Saheeh that the Messenger of Allāh 🌸 said, "A Muhrim should not marry, nor to be married and neither proposed to."

Imām Abū Haneefah 🌸 views that it is permissible to marry during the state of Ihrām. His evidence is the Hadeeth recorded by Imām Bukhāri 🌸 and Imām Muslim 🌸 in their Saheeh, that the Messenger of Allāh 🌸 married Sayyidah Maimoonah 🌸 whilst he was in the state of Ihrām and consummated the marriage after becoming Halāl (i.e. out of Ihrām).

These three examples illustrate some complexities involved when interpreting and inferring rules from the sources of Sharī'ah, despite the evidences being rigorously authentic. The verse about Wudhu, explicates the fact that Wudhu is a pre-requisite for Salāh if one is in need of renewing it as is unanimously agreed by all. The detailed discussion about the integral acts in Wudhu has led to subsequent differences between the jurists solely on the connotation of the letter 'waw'.

The third example, marrying in the state of Ihrām, is a clear example of two rigorously authentic evidences conflicting each other. Both Imāms have their respective views with supporting evidences and juristic principles of preferring one evidence over the other, the details of which are beyond the scope of this discussion. So none of the respective Imāms are to be condemned for differing, especially if their respective opinions are supported with valid and sound evidences and reasoning.

There are literally hundreds of such examples in the Sunnah, in respect to the elaborated discourse of Islamic law such as purity, Zakāt, fasting, Hajj, marriage, divorce, Islamic finance and so forth, in which the four great Imāms have differed. The discussion of each subject area is extensive and exhaustive that requires a lifetime commitment in attempting to analyse the evidences of the opposing views between the scholars with their juristic principles, Usūl ul-Fiqh (legal principles) and criteria of preferences and thereafter to draw decisive and cohesive conclusion.

It is in this respect that we chose to adopt Taqleed - adherence to one of the four Madhabs. Each legal school comprises of reputable jurists and experts in their own right who have dedicated a significant portion of their life to the field of refining and distilling the Sharī'ah for the subsequent generations of the Ummah. It is this refinement process and systemization which facilitates the Ummah to practice their Deen. So, in essence, the prime objective of every Muslim, which is to follow the command of Allāh ﷻ and His Messenger ﷺ, is attained by resorting to one of the four Madhabs.

5: Proofs from the Authentic Sources

Now that the meaning of Taqleed has become clear, some textual evidences will be discussed, explaining the obligation of following and relying on the people of knowledge (Ulamā) in matters of Deen. This will demonstrate that a layperson is not permitted to embark on the task of inferring rules from the Sharī'ah sources without adequate qualifications. Deducing injunctions in matters which one has very little knowledge of, results in misrepresentation of the sacred texts. The inevitable outcome of such an attitude will lead to misguidance and defeat the objective of following the Qur'ān and Sunnah. Some Qur'anic verses will be presented to demonstrate this, followed by Prophetic Ahādeeth;

5.1 Qur'ān

يَا أَيُّهَا الَّذِينَ آمَنُوا أَطِيعُوا اللّهَ وَأَطِيعُوا الرَّسُولَ وَأُولِي الْأَمْرِ مِنْكُمْ

1. "O Believers! Obey Allāh, the Messenger and those authorities amongst you." (4:59)

According to the interpretation of Sayyidunā Jābir Ibn Abdullāh ؓ and Sayyidunā Abdullāh Ibn Abbās ؓ **"Those of authorities..."** implies to the jurists and scholars. (*Ahkāmul Qur'ān vol 2, p.210*)

Some people object that according to the backdrop of the revelation, this verse implies to obeying the leaders as opposed to the jurists and scholars. In response to this, the prime objective of following authorities is to ensure one is following the commandments of Allāh ﷻ and His Messenger ﷺ. The leaders who themselves follow the Sharī'ah in its entirety and are able to resort to the sources, must be followed. This can equally apply to the Mujtahids also, as suggested by the above Companions. Had the verse been restricted to leaders only, then there would have been no scope of eminent Sahābah such as Sayyidunā Abdullāh Ibn Abbās ؓ to interpret otherwise.

وَلَوْ رَدُّوهُ إِلَى الرَّسُولِ وَإِلَى أُولِي الْأَمْرِ مِنْهُمْ لَعَلِمَهُ الَّذِينَ يَسْتَنْبِطُونَهُ مِنْهُمْ وَلَوْلَا فَضْلُ اللهِ
عَلَيْكُمْ وَرَحْمَتُهُ لَاتَّبَعْتُمُ الشَّيْطَانَ إِلَّا قَلِيلًا

2. **"Had they referred the matter to the Messenger and those of authority amongst them, then surely those who infer the matter [by investigating] would come to know of it." (3:83)**

Inferring matters by investigation can also apply to Qiyās (analogical deduction) and Ijtihād in contemporary cases. This is only possible for those who are qualified and possess profound insight into such matters.

(Ahkāmul Qur'ān vol 2, p.262, Roohul Ma'āni vol 5, p.85)

This verse emphatically alerts the layman to resort to expert opinion in matters they have no knowledge of, especially in matters of Ijtihād and ambiguous texts. There are endless cases in jurisprudence where the jurists have differed amongst themselves. Each jurist infers a ruling based on his qualified interpretation of the detail evidences, in light of his Usūl ul-Fiqh.

It is not possible for the layperson to distinguish between sound and weak evidences. Consequently, he will brand others to be wrong whilst considering his interpretation to be the most sound. This is the approach and attitude of many so-called practicing youths today.

A jurist's opinion that conflicts with an authentic Hadeeth, does not mean he has discarded the Sunnah. The jurist may have other supporting evidences and reasons for not acting upon a particular

Hadeeth, as was illustrated in the previous examples (*Classifications of Texts*).

To summarise, the above verse suggests that those who possess knowledge and the right tools of inferring legal rulings are vested with the authority to disclose the law of Allāh ﷻ through intense research of the Shar'ee sources.

فَاسْأَلُوا أَهْلَ الذِّكْرِ إِن كُنتُمْ لَا تَعْلَمُونَ

3: **"So ask the people of knowledge if you do not know."(16:43)**

Allāmah Ālūsi ﷸ, a renowned commentator of the Qur'ān, comments under this verse,

"There are those who have permitted Taqleed of a Mujtahid from this verse, stating that if a person is not a Mujtahid, it becomes mandatory upon him to follow and resort to a Mujtahid scholar due to the command '**So ask..** and the correct position is that there is no distinction (in following) between theological or juristic matters and a Mujtahid whether he is alive or deceased'"

(Roohul Ma'āni vol 7, p.387)

This verse with its commentary is self-explanatory, suggesting the obligation of a layman to resort to the view of a Mujtahid in matters pertaining to the Deen.

5.2. Hadeeth

1: Sayyidunā Hudhaifah ﷺ relates that the Messenger of Allāh ﷺ said, "*I do not know how long I will remain with you, so follow these two people after me; Abū Bakr and Umar."*(Tirmizi)

2: The Messenger of Allāh ﷺ is reported to have said in regards to Sayyidunā Abdullāh Ibn Mas'ood ؓ, *"I am pleased with you for what the son of Umm Abd [i.e. Abdullāh Ibn Mas'ood] is pleased with you."*(Mustadrak)

3: The Messenger of Allāh ﷺ sent Sayyidunā Mu'ādh ؓ to Yemen as a governor and a teacher. The Messenger of Allāh ﷺ posed certain questions to ascertain his method of judging between people. He began by asking him how he would judge if a matter was presented to him. Sayyidunā Mu'ādh ؓ replied, "With the Book of Allāh." He asked, "What if you don't find it in the Book of Allāh ﷻ?" He replied, "Then from the Sunnah." He asked, "What if you do not find it in the Sunnah?" He responded, "Then I will apply Ijtihād."The Messenger of Allāh ﷺ patted him on his chest [as a gesture of ratification] and remarked, "Praise be to Allāh who has enabled the messenger [i.e. Mu'ādh] of the Messenger of Allāh, for that which the Messenger of Allāh is pleased with."

(Abū Dāwood)

In the first Hadeeth, the Messenger of Allāh ﷺ instructed the Companions to follow Sayyidunā Abū Bakr ؓ and Sayyidunā Umar ؓ in matters pertaining to Deen. Following them is tantamount to following the Holy Prophet ﷺ in all religious affairs. Some argue that this Hadeeth only refers to pledging allegiance of their Khilāfah on earth. In reality, a Khaleefah's role is not just restricted to the political administration but also extends to resolving judicial matters. Both Khaleefahs possessed the competency of Ijtihād and are reported to have solved many judicial matters during their time. The fact that they were in a position of issuing legal verdicts and the masses followed their legal opinions, evidently suggests the importance of resorting to experts in matters relating to legal opinions.

The second and third Hadeeth refer to two significant personalities possessing immense knowledge, both of whom were dispatched not only to govern but as teachers and authorities in legal matters. Sayyidunā Abdullāh Ibn Mas'ood ؓ was sent as a teacher for the people in Kūfa, in Iraq during the reign of Sayyidunā Umar ؓ and Sayyidunā Mu'ādh ؓ was sent to Yemen during the time of the Messenger of Allāh ﷺ as a governor and teacher. Both Companions were possessors of immense knowledge in their own right. The Messenger of Allāh ﷺ referred to Sayyidunā Mu'ādh Ibn Jabal ؓ as the possessor of the knowledge of Halāl and Harām and about Sayyidunā Abdullāh Ibn Mas'ood ؓ, he bequeathed to his Companions to accept whatever he says as true. When both were sent to their respective provinces to teach people, the community entrusted their religious affairs to them and exclusively relied on their legal verdicts.

To illustrate this further, Aswad Ibn Yazeed ؓ relates, "Mu'ādh Ibn Jabal ؓ was sent to us as a teacher or a governor [the narrator is unsure as to which word was used] to Yemen. We enquired from him about a man who has passed away and left behind his daughter and his sister [the manner in which the wealth will be distributed between them]. He gave half [of the estate] to the daughter and the remaining half to the sister." (Bukhāri)

Regarding Sayyidunā Abdullāh Ibn Mas'ood 🙴, Imām Bukhāri 🙵 records an incident in his Saheeh that once some people approached Sayyidunā Abū Mūsa al-Ash'ari 🙴 enquiring about an issue related to inheritance. He answered their query but referred them to Sayyidunā Abdullāh Ibn Mas'ood 🙴 (to seek confirmation of his answer). When Sayyidunā Abdullāh Ibn Mas'ood 🙴 responded to their query, they discovered that his response was different from the answer of Sayyidunā Abū Mūsa 🙴. They re-approached Sayyidunā Abū Mūsa 🙴 to inform him of his fellow Companion's answer. Upon hearing Sayyidunā Abdullāh's 🙴 answer, he remarked, "Do not ask me anything as long as this great scholar [Abdullāh Ibn Mas'ood 🙴] is present amongst you."

The preceding evidences make it clear that the practice of adhering to the Fatwa of an expert and relying on their expertise, without the need of demanding evidence has existed since the first generation of Muslims. This approach is in actual fact similar to Taqleed Shakhsi.

4: The Messenger of Allāh 🙵 said, *"Verily the cure for ignorance is to question."* (Abū Dāwood)

The wordings of the above Hadeeth suggests to every common reader that the most appropriate and correct approach to seeking knowledge and dispel ignorance is to question, but questions must be posed to those who are considered experts in the field. Passing a judgement without prior investigation of the matter, nor consulting those in positions of authority is a grave sin. The Messenger of Allāh 🙵 would reprimand and disapprove of those passing judgement without sound knowledge or without consulting the people of knowledge. This is clearly demonstrated from the background incident that occurred which caused the Holy Prophet ﷺ to make the above statement.

Sayidunā Jābir ﷺ relates, "We went on a journey and one of the Companions amongst us was struck with a rock that injured his head (severely). He had a wet dream (which required him to perform a ritual bath but due to the excruciating pain on the wound, passing water over it was difficult). He consulted the Companions to seek for the dispensation of Tayammum (dry ablution). They replied, "We do not find any dispensation for you because you are able to use water." The Companion thus performed a ritual bath and died (as a result of this). When we came to the Messenger of Allāh ﷺ and informed him of this account, he remarked (as though he was angry), "They killed him, may Allāh destroy them! Why did they not ask if they did not know? <u>Verily the cure for ignorance is to question</u>. It would have sufficed him if he had done a dry ablution and kept his wound bandaged." (Baihaqi)

Despite the fact that the Companions issued a ruling based on their understanding, the Messenger of Allāh ﷺ held them responsible for the tragic death of their comrade because of not consulting the matter before hand and failing to understand the matter properly. The Messenger of Allāh's ﷺ rebuke of his Companions becomes apparent from the words, "Qātalahumullāh (may Allāh destroy them)." The notion of 'do it yourself' or 'seek the answers for yourself by going back to the Qur'ān and Sunnah' is refuted by this single incident. If this attitude will not lead to misapplications of the

Divine laws then what will it not do?

The forthcoming evidences shall illustrate some more examples of following the opinions of legal experts.

5.3. The Existence of Taqleed Shakhsi During the Era of the Sahābah 📿

1: Ikrimah 📿 relates that [during the season of Hajj] a group of people from Madeenah enquired from Ibn Abbās 📿, the ruling regarding a woman who starts to menstruate during the first Tawāf [prior to the final Tawāf]. He said that she is permitted to go home without completing the final Tawāf. The people of Madeenah remarked, "We shall not prefer your opinion over the opinion of Zaid Ibn Thābit" (Bukhāri). In another narration recorded in the Musnad of Abū Dāwood Tayālisi, reported from Qatādah 📿 (a Tābi'ee scholar), the words used were, "We will not follow you, O Ibn Abbās as you go against the opinion of Zaid."

The above is a clear illustration of strict adherence to the opinion of a reputable jurist whilst leaving the opinion of another equally reputable jurist.

At this point, it can be argued that Sayyidunā Zaid Ibn Thābit 📿 was accredited to be an authority and one of the leading jurists in Madeenah. He was a pioneering figure, responsible for the dissemination of knowledge in Madeenah after the demise of the Messenger of Allāh 📿. Many reputable Companions and other local residents preferred his legal verdicts over others, as in the above case.

This is apparent from Ibnul Qayyim Al-Jawziyyah's 🕮 statement;

" It is said that Ibn Umar ⚜ and a group of those who lived after him in Madeenah amongst the Companions ⚜ of the Messenger of Allāh 🕮 used to issue verdicts according to what they acquired from the Madhab of Zaid Ibn Thābit ⚜, in those matters which they did not memorise from the Messenger of Allāh's 🕮 statements." (*I'lāmul Mooqi'een vol 1, p.17*)

This is similar to the practice of Taqleed Shakhsi, so if this was the case during that era, referred to as the golden era, then how important is it for the Muslims today to adhere to one of the four accredited schools?

2: Amr Ibn Maimoon al-Awdai 🕮, a Tābi'ee, relates, "Mu'ādh Ibn Jabal ⚜ came to us in Yemen as a messenger of the Messenger of Allāh 🕮. I heard his Takbeer during Fajr and noticed the deepness of his voice. I began developing a keen interest towards him so I (remained in his company and) did not depart from his company until I buried him in Syria. I then began searching for the most knowledgeable person after him and thus, came to discover Abdullāh Ibn Mas'ood ⚜ (to be the most knowledgeable). So I remained in his company until he died." (Abū Dāwood)

Intriguingly, inspite that there were many prominent Companions ⚜ existing, the narrator relates his strong attachment to an individual Companion for gaining Islamic knowledge and relying on their Islamic scholarship. Any student of Deen choosing to seek knowledge from an individual teacher, like in this case, would give preference to his teacher's views and interpretation of the sacred Islamic law over others, due to his prolonged attachment with that teacher. In the similar manner, a Muqallid (follower) adheres to a particular school of thought and their methodological framework of interpretation of the juristic laws. He thus, prefers their qualified scholarship over others.

6. Evolvement Period of Taqleed

6.1. Era of the Sahābah ؓ

The practice of Taqleed Shakhsi can be retrospectively traced back to the era of the Sahābah ؓ and Tābi'een ؓ. In actual fact, practicing Taqleed is an avenue of following the path of the pious predecessors, the Salafs. Nevertheless, strict adherence was not made compulsory in the beginning because there was no fear of one following their desires and misrepresentation of the Deen as opposed to today. The questions that arise are then, (1) How did the four major schools, Hanafi, Shāfi'ee, Māliki and Hanbali schools emerge and gain recognition throughout the world and, (2) Why did Taqleed Shakhsi of these schools only become necessary? To answer these two questions, first a brief historical analysis of the evolvement of Taqleed will be discussed.

After the demise of the Holy Prophet ﷺ, the Companions ؓ advanced beyond the Arab Peninsula and conquered the territories of the Persian and the Roman Empires. Within a period of thirty years, the Muslims conquered the region of Shām, Egypt, Iraq, Iran, North Africa and the Persian Gulf as well as other surrounding provinces, all of which became part of the extended Islamic empire. Consequently, a significant number of the Sahābah ﷺ dispersed throughout the conquered lands and took residency there whilst many chose to remain in Makkah and Madeenah. Many of them took positions of authority and governed certain regions for instance, Sayyidunā Amr Ibn Ās ﷺ governed the entire Egypt, Sayyidunā Mu'āwiyah ﷺ governed the entire Shām and so on. In addition to political administration, many also assumed roles of teachers and imparted Islamic knowledge to the local citizens. Subsequently, they became legal consultants as well as political leaders for those local people.

Though the Companions ﷺ acquired their knowledge directly under the tutelage of the Messenger of Allāh ﷺ, they differed amongst themselves in the detailed aspects of Islamic Law, especially in those instances where no clear textual evidence were to be found. These differences were mainly due to the different level of understanding and knowledge. To give an example, the Qur'ān clearly states that a woman who becomes widowed whilst not being pregnant must observe a waiting period of four months and ten days instantly after the demise of her husband. However, the Holy Qur'ān also recalls in another place that the waiting period of a pregnant woman is until she delivers her child, irrespective of the duration period that remains for her delivery.

So, in a hypothetical situation, if a woman's husband dies whist she is carrying a child then which of the above two waiting periods must she observe; four months and ten days or until delivering the child? Sayyidunā Ali ﷺ viewed that she will observe the longer of the two period in order to incorporate both commands. Hence, if pregnancy is the longest of the two period then she must observe the waiting period of pregnancy. If not then four months and ten days. However, Sayyidunā Abdullāh Ibn Mas'ood ؓ viewed that the verse of pregnancy is a generic command applying to all instances, thus if she is pregnant, her period will expire the moment she gives birth irrespective of whether she delivers the child in less than four months and ten days, after her husband's death.

This is an example of two profound and knowledgeable Companions ؓ differing in regards to a Qur'anic injunction. This reflects on their different level of understanding and interpreting the Islamic law based on sound reasoning. Other reasons of differences amongst the Companions ؓ included, identification of the *illat* (effective course), acceptance of a Hadeeth, application of Hadeeth whereby one Companion applied it in one instance whilst another Companion applied it elsewhere, whether a command is abrogated or not and also, different location. Each of the above reasons require an extensive discussion which is beyond the scope of our discussion.

Another example of differences amongst the Companions ؓ is the distribution of the conquered lands in Iraq and Syria, whether they should be distributed amongst the Muslim soldiers as spoils of war or remain in the possession of their respective owners. This required extensive Ijtihād and critical analysis in searching for a precedented example from the Qur'ān and Sunnah. The Qur'ān only instructs one-fifth of the spoils of war to be allotted for the poor and destitute people, but has remained silent about the distribution of the remaining four parts. This issue led to two groups;

The first group viewed that they should be included as part of the spoils of war, thus the Muslim soldiers should receive a share of those lands. Amongst those who opined this position were Sayyiduna Abdur Rahmān Ibn Auf ؓ and Sayyiduna Bilāl ؓ. Their supporting evidence was that in the fourth year after migration, the Messenger of Allāh ﷺ distributed the lands belonging to the Banū Nadheer (a Jewish tribe initially residing in Madeenah) after evicting them from Madeenah because of their treason. After assigning one-fifth of the share for charity, according to the Qur'ān [8:41], the Messenger of Allāh ﷺ distributed the remaining four parts between the Muslim soldiers. Two years after this incident, the land of Khaybar was conquered in which the Messenger of Allāh ﷺ distributed some parts of the lands between the Muslim soldiers.

On the other hand, the second group which included Sayyiduna Umar ؓ, Sayyiduna Uthmān ؓ and Sayyiduna Mu'ādh Ibn Jabal ؓ opined that those lands should remain in the possession of the land owners and not be distributed as part of the spoils of war. Their supporting evidence was that in the eighth year after migration, the Muslims conquered Makkah, but without any major encountering with the enemies. The Messenger of Allāh ﷺ did not distribute their lands amongst the Muslim soldiers and allowed those lands to be retained by their owners. Furthermore, the Messenger of Allāh ﷺ allowed some portion of land in Khaybar to remain in the hands of their owners after its conquest. This suggests that it is not mandatory for the leader to dispense the remaining four parts amongst the soldiers. If he wants, he may allow the landowners to retain their lands.

From the forgoing example, both groups of Companions ﷺ referred to the same Qur'anic verse that speaks of the spoils of war but reached to two different conclusions. Each group interpreted it in accordance to their observation and understanding from the practice of the Messenger of Allāh ﷺ.

This discussion illustrates that the Companions of great scholarship exercised Ijtihād in new cases by resorting to the Qur'ān and Sunnah in search for similitude examples. Consequently, this lead them to differ amongst themselves in legal matters since each Companion concludes with a ruling based on his personal investigation, interpretation and analysis. Such differences, paved the foundation for Ijtihādic differences in non-textual and unclear matters in the subsequent generations.

By the end of the second era, two interpretive schools were ingrained; the first being the school of Hadeeth in Madeenah and Makkah pioneered by Companions ﷺ such as Sayyidunā Abdullāh Ibn Umar ﷺ, Sayyidunā Abū Hurairah ﷺ and others and the second one being the school of Ijtihād which reigned in Kūfa, pioneered by Sayyidunā Abdullāh Ibn Mas'ood ﷺ, Sayyidunā Ali ﷺ and other Companions ﷺ who took residency in Iraq.

In contrast to Madeenah and Makkah, the Companions ﷺ living in Iraq encountered innumerable complex issues which they had never faced before, such as the example above, requiring them to exercise extensive Ijtihād. These complex issues included new cultures, influx conversion of non-Arabs into Islām, emergence of deviant sects and fabricators of Hadeeth which required strict conditions for accepting Hadeeth and much more. Madeenah and Makkah, on the other hand, were secured from such complicated matters because most of them were already solved during the lifetime of the Messenger of Allāh ﷺ and Sayyidunā Abū Bakr ﷺ. Access to Hadeeth was much easier in Makkah and Madeenah and its transmitter(s) required less scrutiny because of the widespread religiousness of people in these two vicinities.

As a result, the residence of these two regions relied heavily on the literal meaning of the Hadeeth and accepted Hadeeth from whoever related it to them. This is not to suggest that the Companions ﷺ in Makkah and Madeenah never employed Ijtihād or condemned it. In some cases they did employ Ijtihād, however in contrast to Kūfa, their employment of Ijtihād was very rare. After the era of the Companions ﷺ, Iraq produced scholars of profound knowledge of Hadeeth and Fiqh such as Alqamah (the student of Abdullāh Ibn Mas'ood ﷺ), Ibrāheem an-Nakha'i ﷺ, Hammād Ibn Abi Sulaimān ﷺ, Qādhi Shuraih ﷺ (a judge appointed by Sayyidunā Umar ﷺ) to name but a few. Their teachings and interpretation of the legal matters in religion served the foundation of legal thought for the residents of Iraq, which was then collated and systemised by Imām Abū Haneefah ﷺ and his students.

6.2. The Period of the Tābi'een and Tabi Tābi'een and the Emergence of the Four Schools

Around the first half of the third century of the Islamic calendar was the period of the four Imāms. The Tāb'een (successors of the Sahābah ﷺ) propagated the knowledge they acquired from the Sahābah ﷺ. The Companions ﷺ differing in the detailed aspects of the Islamic Law inevitably led the successors to differ as well, which brought about many schools of opinions.

Initially, there were many schools of thought operating in other regions such as the Madhab of Abū Layth ﷺ in northern Iraq, Imām Awza'i ﷺ in Syria, Imām Hasan al-Basri ﷺ in Basra (Iraq) and so on. However, they did not enjoy the same privilege as that of the four major schools of thought did. Over the passage of time, the students of each of the four Imāms began developing and transmitting their Ijtihādic principles to the subsequent generations. The subsequent students initiated the compilation of literatures dealing with detailed Fiqhi (juristic) cases, relating to matters pertaining to every facet of human life, which encompassed the laws of purity, devotional matters, commercial finance, marriage, divorce, penal laws, inheritance and so on. Their *Usūl ul-Fiqh* (legal theories) were codified and served as an interpretive model for the Sharī'ah sources.

The leading pioneers of each of the four schools are;

1. Imām Abū Haneefah ﷺ (b.80 - d.150 AH)
2. Imām Mālik Ibn Anas ﷺ (b.93 – d.179 AH)
3. Imām Muhammad Ibn Idrees Ash-Shāfi'ee ﷺ (b.150 – d.204 AH)
4. Imām Ahmad Ibn Hanbal ﷺ (b.164 – d.241 AH)

6.3. The Period of Codification and the Scholars' Adherence to One of the Four Imāms

The period between the third and the fourth century of the Islamic calendar marked the perfect moment for subsequent scholars to further develop, refine and preserve the juristic works by codifying and composing books of commentaries. The scholars eventually adopted their methodological framework and disseminated that legal framework and jurisprudence throughout the region they resided in. Many of the existing schools were gradually replaced by one of the four schools. Hence, the adherents to the Awza'i school of thought in Syria for instance, struggled to resolve new cases, they borrowed laws from the newly developed Shāfi'ee school. Similarly, adherents to the Basri school in Basra borrowed laws from the Hanafi school in Kūfa to resolve newly emerging cases. In this way, the other schools ceased to exist and were replaced.

Scholars of great calibre in the subsequent generation attached themselves to one of the four schools and contributed to the preservation and expansion of their school. Each school comprised of hundreds and thousands of adherent scholars, each one being a specialist in his own right either in Tafseer, Hadeeth, Fiqh, Arabic Grammar, Arabic Linguistic and Rhetoric or Tasawwuf. If a non-Muqallid (one who does not practice Taqleed), chooses to discard the credibility of the four schools by abandoning the adherence of one of them, under the pretext of strictly following the Qur'ān and Sunnah. Then in response to this, it could be argued that history has produced many calibre of scholars with great academic credentials who adhered to one of the four legal schools.

Some of the unquestionable personalities who practiced Taqleed of one of the four Imāms after their demise are as follows;

1.   Imām Abū Easa At-Tirmizi (Shāfi'ee) ﷺ – a Muhaddith
2.   Imām Yahya Ibn Ma'een (Hanafi) ﷺ – a Muhaddith
3.   Imām Baihaqi (Shāfi'ee) ﷺ – a Muhaddith
4.   Imām Abū Jafar At-Tahāwi ﷺ (Hanafi) - a Muhaddith and Faqeeh
5.   Imām Fakhr ud-Deen Ar-Rāzi ﷺ (Shāfi'ee) – a Mufassir
6.   Imām Ibn Abdul-Barr ﷺ (Māliki) – a Muhaddith
7.   Imām Abū Zakariyya An-Nawāwi ﷺ (Shāfi'ee) – a Muhaddith and Faqeeh
8.   Imām Abū Bakr Jassās ﷺ (Hanafi) – a Mufassir and Faqeeh
9.   Imām Ibn Rajab ﷺ (Hanbali) – a Faqeeh
10.   Imām Ibn ul-Humām ﷺ (Hanafi) – a Faqeeh
11.   Imām Abū Ishāq Ash-Shātibi ﷺ (Māliki) – a Faqeeh
12.   Imām Ibn Hajr Al-Asqalāni ﷺ (Shāfi'ee) – a Muhaddith
13.   Imām Abūl-Abbās Al-Qurtubi ﷺ (Māliki) – a Mufassir
14.   Imām Badr ud-Deen Al-Ayni ﷺ (Hanafi) – a Muhaddith
15.   Imām Jalāl ud-Deen As-Suyūti ﷺ (Shāfi'ee) – a Mufassir, Muhaddith and a master in almost every field
16.   Imām Ibn Rushd ﷺ (Māliki) – a Faqeeh
17.   Imām Adh-Dhahabi ﷺ (Shāfi'ee) – a Muhaddith and an authority in Asmā-ur-Rijāl (critical analysis of the narrators in the chain of transmission)
18.   Imām Ibn Qudāmah ﷺ (Hanbali) – a Faqeeh
19.   Imām Abū Hāmid Al-Ghazāli ﷺ (Shāfi'ee) – a Saint, Faqeeh and Theologian

20. Ibn Ābideen Ash-Shāmi ﷺ (Hanafi) – a Faqeeh
21. Ibn Katheer ﷺ (Shāfi'ee) – a Mufassir and Historian

Some have argued that there are established cases in which erudite scholars, such as those mentioned above have differed from the opinions of their own Imāms. For instance, Imām Abū Yūsuf ﷺ and Imām Muhammad ﷺ have differed with Imām Abū Haneefah ﷺ on many instances. This is also the case with scholars belonging to other schools of thought, hence their strict adherence to the school is not established.

In response to this argument, though undoubtedly it is true that scholars have differed with their respective Imāms on many in-stances, but these differences were based on Ijtihādic differences in the elaborated Fiqhi discourses. The erudite scholars were famous for adhering to the juristic principles and legal theories of one of the four schools, not necessarily in strict adherence to every Fiqhi case. The scholars were well-rooted in their juristic principles and the science of Ijtihād, giving them the dispensation to divert from the view of the Imām on certain issues in the discourse of Fiqh, if they deemed another evidence to be stronger in their view. Never-theless, the fact that they embraced the legal principles of their Imām and utilised them for deducing and interpreting laws does not take them out of the Madhab completely.

(Ibn Ābideen Ash-Shāmi, *Rasmul Mufti*, p.36)

However, for a layperson to investigate by searching through the entire elaborated discourse of Fiqh and juristic principles exten-sively to determine which is the most closest to the Sunnah, is beyond his capacity. He has not even grasped the basics of the legal principles of interpreting the Shari'ah leave aside determining which of the two positions is the most strongest. A layperson must therefore, practice Taqleed to avoid further confusion and the risk of misrepresenting the Deen.

7. Why did Talqeed Shakhsi Become Necessary?

Evil desire is one of the most influential and momentous force that constantly provokes and lures man into sin. In a lengthy Hadeeth recorded in the Sunan of Ibn Mājah, the Messenger of Allāh ﷺ prophesised that the following of desires would prevail and that every self-opinioned man will be obsessed with his own opinion. This obviously refers to that person who without any sound knowledge and proper qualification voices his own opinion on certain issues (related to Islām) and then becomes obsessed by it. In other reports, the Messenger of Allāh ﷺ prophesised the emergence of a group who would issue verdicts without sound knowledge. As a result, they will be misguided and end up misguiding others.

The egos and desires of a man is a powerful instrument which the devil uses to his advantage to destroy mankind. This can manifest in many forms, amongst of which is being selective in ones own Deen by picking and choosing whatever deems favourable. If a layperson is presented with conflicting evidences and opposing views of the scholars without acknowledging the evidences of both sides nor understanding the principles behind of preferring the strongest of the two conflicting evidences, he will inevitably succumb to his desires by selecting the most favourable position under the pretext of following the Qur'ān and Sunnah.

A typical example of two opposing views is that according to the Shāfi'ee school, the flowing of blood does not invalidate the Wudhu whereas physical touching of a woman invalidates the Wudhu. The Hanafi school views the vice-versa, that physical touching of a woman does not invalidate the Wudhu but flowing of blood invalidates it. At this point, a non-Muqallid layman's first argument will be to follow the Hadeeth. However, both Imāms have arrived to their respective conclusions based on Hadeeth. His next argument will then be to follow that which is the soundest of the two. The counter argument will then be that on what basis will he determine the soundness of a Hadeeth if he is not equipped with the science of Hadeeth? Each Imām has arrived to his own conclusion based on the soundest of the two evidences according to him. If his response is to give preference to Bukhāri and Muslim over other Hadeeth, then to this we reply that none of the classical jurists have included in their juristic principles to prefer Bukhāri and Muslim over the rest.

Bukhāri and Muslim are undoubtedly ranked as the highest compilations of authentic Ahādeeth. Nevertheless, this approach will ensue in discrediting all of the other authentic Ahādeeth contained in other large collections. The soundness of Hadeeth is not determined by which collection it contains, rather determined by the transmitters in the chain. It is probable that a Hadeeth contained in another collection, for instance the Muwatta of Imām Malik ؓ is more rigorously authentic than a Hadeeth in Bukhāri and Muslim since its chain of transmitters from the author to the Holy Prophet ﷺ is far less in comparison to the chain of transmitters in Bukhāri and Muslim. Furthermore, Mujtahid scholars have differed in respect to accepting or rejecting a Hadeeth since the criteria of one Mujtahid may differ from the others. So, will a non-Muqallid be able to choose the most correct position on this matter?

If he proposes the argument that he will follow the opinion of such and such scholar then is that not Taqleed in essence? Would he question the credibility of the scholar and his way of interpreting the Hadeeth or his method of inference?

Another resort the non-Muqallid may choose is to be selective in his approach by taking the easiest of the options on the premise that all four Imāms are correct. He will follow the Hanafi position in the intactness of Wudhu when touching a female and also the Shāfi'ee position in the intactness of the Wudhu with the flowing of blood. However, if he performs Salāh in this manner, then his Wudhu and Salāh are considered invalid according to both Imāms. Though he may argue his case of following the Hadeeth or that all four Imāms are correct, his standpoint on this matter has been dictated by his desires.

The final option available for him is to adhere to a particular Madhab that comprises of erudite scholars, specialised in various sciences and to follow their interpretive model and juristic principles which have been tried, tested and approved by scholars throughout centuries. In this way, his ego is controlled and will also follow Qur'ān and Sunnah in a systematic and coherent manner.

The scholars of the past therefore issued a consensus for the general masses not equipped with the tools of Ijtihād to follow one of the four major schools of thought to prevent the Deen from being misrepresented or employed to suite ones personal desires and satisfaction. Imām Shihāb ud-Deen An-Nafrawi ﷺ a Māliki scholar reports a consensus of all the scholars that Taqleed Shaksī - following one of the four schools, is necessary;

"The consensus of the Muslims has been established upon the Wujūb (obligation) of following one of the four Imāms today; Abū Haneefah, Mālik, Shāfi'ee and Ahmad, (may Allāh ﷻ be pleased with them). What we explained before, in terms of the obligation of following one of the four Imāms, is in relation to those who do not possess the capability of performing Ijtihād."(Al-Fawākih Ad-Dawāni, vol.2 p.574)

The Hanbali scholar, Imām 'Alā ud-Deen Al-Mardawi ﷺ cites the statement of the famous scholar Imām Al-Wazeer Ibn Hubaira:

"Consensus has been established upon Taqleed of one of the four schools and that the truth does not lie outside of them."

(Al-Insāf, Vol.11 p.169)

8. Why Choose Taqleed of the Four Schools?

Muslims living in the West are responsible for representing and propagating Islām in its purest form. This is only achievable if one follows the teachings of the pious predecessors and appreciates their methodological framework of interpreting the Sharī'ah. As was indicated previously, one of the most remarkable achievements of the surviving four legal schools was the subsequent development of their legal and juristic framework. Scholars of great academic ability and scholarship embraced their systematic framework and gave them worldwide recognition. The four surviving schools were able to resolve textual complexities and virtually find solutions to innumerable unsolved issues in every generation. This increased the robustness of the four schools, enabling them to shun the doors of excessive numbers of opinions on one single issue.

Had there not been a consensus upon adhering to one of the four schools, there would have been hundreds of Madhabs by now. This would have then, opened a floodgate of more Madhabs and diversity within the Ummah. The Muslim community will thus have failed to present Islām in a coherent and a pure manner. Following one of the four schools is what united the people together in the past. Irrespective of the differences of opinions that existed between them in jurisprudential matters, they were considered as valid differences.

The Messenger of Allāh ﷺ himself ratified differences amongst the Sahābah ؓ if the intention was to uphold the commands of Allāh ﷻ and His Messenger ﷺ in its purest form. To give an example of this, once the Messenger of Allāh ﷺ instructed his Companions ؓ to advance towards the quarters of Banū Quraidha (a Jewish tribe) and lay siege to them because of their act of treason. The Messenger of Allāh ﷺ gave them clear instructions that no one should perform Asr Salāh except at Banū Quraidha. The narrator states that whilst they were on their way, the time for Asr Sālah was coming to an end. The Companions 🙵 began discussing whether they should pray Asr Salāh on the way or not. This subsequently led to them forming two groups. The first group insisted on performing Salāh on the way fearing the possibility of becoming Qadhā. They interpreted the statement of the Messenger of Allāh 🙵 to mean that they should advance quickly in order to reach there before Asr time expires. The second group insisted on performing Asr Salāh at Banū Quraidha regardless if its time expires, taking the command as being literal. Both groups acted upon their own interpretation and then presented this matter to the Messenger of Allāh 🙵. Upon hearing the reasoning from both parties, the Messenger of Allāh 🙵 endorsed both practices and did not reprimand anyone because he acknowledged their sincerity and eagerness in fulfilling the command of Allāh 🙵 and His Messenger 🙵.

Each of the four Imāms has an unbroken chain stretching back to the Prophet 🙵. Although the four legal schools differed in legal issues, each one strove with sincere efforts in propagating what they believed was closest to the truth. The later scholars acknowledged their differences of opinions. Imām Suyūti 🙵 said: "The difference found in the four schools in this nation is a huge blessing and an enormous virtue. It has a subtle hidden wisdom that the intelligent are able to grasp, but the ignorant are blind of. I have even heard some of them say: 'The Prophet 🙵 came with one law, so where did the four Madhabs come from?"

Inspite of their differences, the scholars converged upon considering their legal principles to be a valid interpretive model of the Shari'ah. Hence following one of the four schools is necessary and to discard them is nothing but opening the doors of more diverse opinions, more confusion and discord amongst the Ummah.

9. The Recognition of the Four Schools Throughout the World.

As discussed previously, the scholars inaugurated the process of codification and transmitted that knowledge to their students, who then transmitted it to their students in Islamic seminaries until today. Many also took positions of authority in certain provinces and issued verdicts according to the opinion of one of the four Imāms. As a result of this, within a century or so, their teachings disseminated and gained recognition throughout the Islamic World. At present, the geographical locations in which these four respective Madhabs operating are;

Hanafi School

Some parts of Egypt and Syria and surrounding regions, Pakistan, India, Bangladesh, Turkey, Afghanistan, Indonesia, Malaysia, Uzbekistan, Iraq, Russia and Western Countries.

Māliki School

Initiated in Madeenah during Imām Mālik's time, North Africa, Egypt, Spain and some areas in Basra.

Shāfi'ee School

Most parts of Egypt, Syria, some parts of Iraq, Sajistan, Palestine, Jordan and most parts of the Middle-Eastern region.

Hanbali School

School initiated in Iraq and Egypt and in the Arab peninsula.

10. The Statements of Scholars on the Necessity of Taqleed Shakhsi

Below are the statements of some of the distinguishing scholars explaining the necessity for Taqleed Shakhsi for a layperson, who has not attained the level of Ijtihād. Inspite of this, astonishingly, the advocates of the abandonment of Taqleed Shakhsi still persist in its condemnation. Some have gone as far as rejecting its consensus amongst the scholars. This is nothing but due to shear ignorance and lack of understanding. Read the statements below to discover for yourself what the scholars have to say on this issue;

1: Imām Shams ud-Deen Dhahabi, known as Hāfiz Ad-Dhahabi ﷺ, states:

"I follow (what I believe to be) the truth and perform Ijtihād (when necessary). I do not adhere to any Madhab, I say: yes. Whoever has reached the level of Ijtihād and a number of Imāms have attested to this regarding him, it is not allowed for him to do Taqleed, just as it is not seeming at all for the beginner layman jurist who has committed the Qur'ān to memory or a great deal of it to perform Ijtihād. How is he going to perform Ijtihād? What will he say? On what grounds shall he base his opinions? How can he fly when his wings have not yet grown?"(*Siyar A'lām un-Nubalā*, Vol.18, Pg.191)

Hāfiz Ad-Dhahabi 🕮 was an undisputed scholar of Hadeeth, due to whom Ibn Hajr Al-Asqalāni 🕮, the commentator of Saheeh al-Bukhāri, aspired to memorise Ahādeeth. Imām Dhahabi has authored over hundreds of works, related to many sciences but mostly in Hadeeth science. His speciality was Hadeeth and was an authority in his own right. One of his famous works existing today is Tazkiratul Huffāz, a voluminous encyclopaedia dealing with the critical analysis of every narrator in the chain and determining whether such a narrator is reliable or not.

2: Allāmah Ibnul Humām 🕮 a renowned Hanafi scholar states:

"(As for the layman) it is obligatory for him to do Taqleed of a single Mujtahid... The jurists have stated that the one who moves from one Madhab to another by his Ijtihād and evidence is sinful deserving of being punished. Thus one who does so without Ijtihād and evidence is even more deserving."(*Fath ul-Qadeer*, the *commentary of Al-Hidāyah, vol.6 p.360*)

3: Imām Nawāwi 🕮, a renowned Shāfi'ee jurist and Muhaddith, states:

"The second view is, it is necessary for him (the layman) to follow one particular school and that was the definitive position according to Imām Abul-Hasan. This applies to everyone who has not reached to the degree of Ijtihād of the jurists and scholars of other disciplines. The reasoning for this ruling is, that if it was permitted to follow any school one wished, it would lead towards selecting the dispensations of the schools and the following of ones desires. He would (eventually) be choosing between Halāl and Harām and obligatory and permissible. This would lead to relinquishing one-self from the burden of responsibility. This is not the same as during the first generations, for the schools that were sufficient in terms of their rulings for newer issues were neither structured nor widespread. Thus, on this basis it is obligatory for a person to strive in choosing a Madhab which alone he follows."

(*Sharh Al-Muhadhdhab*, Vol.1 p.93)

4: Imām Sha'rāni ☙, an authority within the Shāfi'ee school states;

"...You (O student) have no excuse left for not doing Taqleed of any Madhab you wish from the schools of the four Imāms, for they are all paths to Heaven..." (*Al-Meezānul-Kubrā*, vol.1 p.55)

5: Imām Salih As-Sunūsi ☙ writes:

"As for the scholar who has not reached the level of Ijtihād and the non-scholar, they must do Taqleed of the Mujtahid... And the most correct view is that it is Wājib (obligatory) to adhere to a particular school from the four schools..." (*Fath al-'Alee al-Mālik fil- Fatwa 'alā Madhab al-Imām Mālik*, p.40-41)

6: Imām Alā ud-Deen Al-Mardawi ☙, a Hanbali scholar, in his major juristic compendium Al-Insāf, records the statement of the famous scholar Imām Al-Wazeer Ibn Hubaira ☙:

"Consensus has been established upon Taqleed of one of the four schools and that the truth does not lie outside of them."

(*Al-Insāf*, Vol.11 p.169)

7: Imām Āmidi ☉ writes in Al-Ahkām fi Usūl ul-Ahkām:

"The layman and anyone who is not capable of Ijtihād, even if he has acquired mastery of some of the sciences related to Ijtihād, is obligated with following the positions of the Mujtahid Imāms and taking their juristic opinions and this is the view of the experts from the scholars of the principles. It was the Mu'tazila of Baghdad who prohibited it, except if the soundness of his Ijtihād becomes clear to him." (*Al-Ahkām fi Usūl ul-Ahkām*, vol.4, p.278)

8: Imām Badr ud-Deen az-Zarkhashi ☉ states; in Al-Bahr ul-Muheet,

"There has been an established consensus amongst the Muslims that the truth is restricted to these (four) schools. Thus it is not permitted to act upon any opinion other than them. Nor is it permitted for Ijtihād to occur except within them (i.e. employing their principles that is the tools of interpretation)." (*Al-Bahrul-Muheet*, vol.6 p.209)

9: Ibn Rajab al-Hanbali ☉ writes;

"...that is the Mujtahid, assuming his existence, his obligation is to follow what becomes apparent to him of the truth. As for the non-Mujtahid his duty is to do Taqleed."

He further states: "As for all other people who have not reached this level (of Ijtihād), it is not allowed for them but to do Taqleed of these four Imāms and to submit to that which the rest of the Ummah submitted to." (*Refutation of Anyone who Follows Other than the Four Schools*, vol.2 p. 626-624)

11. The Principle of Blocking the Means

Taqleed Shakhsi can be proven from a juristic point of view also. It was discussed previously and explained by the statements of the scholars, that Taqleed was made compulsory upon the one who has not attained the level of Ijtihād. This was in order to shun the doors of the influx number of opinions and Madhabs in the Deen and more importantly, to prevent hand-picking between Madhabs based on ones personal desires and satisfaction. In the juristic principle this is known as *Saddun lidharāi* – blocking the means. In other words, the precursory acts that directly lead to sinning are also prohibited so that one does not eventually fall into sin.

For instance, it is common knowledge that Islām has prohibited fornication. Those factors that serve as a precursor towards committing fornication such as casting unlawful gazes at a non-Mahram, free interaction between male and female strangers, unnecessary touching and casual conversation are also prohibited. In the similar light, Allāh ﷻ has prohibited the servant from following his desires. This manifests in different forms, amongst which is being selective in the Deen by always choosing the easiest option between Madhabs, without any academic credentials for personal satisfaction. This attitude of picking and choosing will inevitably corrupt ones religion reducing it to a mere game and abuse. To prevent such abuse from happening to ones religion, to control ones ego and most importantly upholding the status of religion as it ought to be upheld, Taqleed Shakhsi was introduced.

12. Responding to Some Commonly Posed Questions

After discussing the main arguments and statements of reputable scholars on the necessity of Taqleed Shakhsi, this discourse will remain incomplete without discussing the common objections posed against Taqleed. Therefore, in this section we present a detailed response to those common questions.

12.1. Is it possible to strictly adhere to Authentic Hadeeth rather than following a Madhab?

One of the most common arguments posed against Taqleed Shakhsi is that if there is Saheeh (authentic) Hadeeth, then what reason is there to follow a Madhab? They often argue that one attains more closeness to the Sunnah by resorting directly to authentic Hadeeth as opposed to following a Madhab because Hadeeth is infallible as opposed to the Imāms who are fallible.

A careful analysis of the above arguments suggests that such people have no true understanding of the science of Hadeeth and the methodological framework of the scholars of the past. As a result of this, they tend to view Islām as plain black and white; that everything is clear, therefore, Islām will be easier just by following Saheeh Hadeeth. The reality of the matter is, that Islamic Law is much more complex than what they assume it is. Had Islamic Law been easy and simple then diverse opinions amongst jurists would not have risen in the first place. Let alone the jurists, the Sahābah ﷺ would not have differed. There would have been no need to compile Hadeeth books dealing with *ikhtilaful Hadeeth* (differences amongst Hadeeth) such as *Sharhul Ma'āni Al-Athār* of Imām Abū Ja'far At-Tahāwi ﷺ.

Scholars have explicitly stated that a Hadeeth to be rigorously authentic is not the only condition for its practice to be compulsory. In addition, to determine its suitability for practice, application and so forth must also be considered. There are many sound Ahādeeth to be found in the Hadeeth collections but cannot be acted upon. For instance there is a Hadeeth which mentions that the Wudhu is breached by touching anything that is cooked on fire. Though the Hadeeth is rigorously authentic, the scholars unanimously agree that this ruling is now abrogated and no longer suitable for practice because of the Hadeeth in which the Messenger of Allāh ﷺ once consumed goats meat (cooked on fire) and thereafter performed Salāh instantly without repeating his Wudhu.

Shaykh Muhammad Al-Awwāmah ﷺ, a renowned Syrian Muhaddith (scholar in Hadeeth) explains that what is meant by acting upon an authentic Hadeeth is that it must be suitable for practice. In addition to a critical assessment of the chain of transmitters and text, other factors must be taken into consideration such as the inference of laws [abrogation] and so on, as opposed to the popular notion that the soundness of the chain is sufficient for its practice to be necessary. (*Atharul Hadeeth Shareef fi Ikhtilāfil A'immatil Fuqahā* [Urdu version] p.98)

In determining the suitability for practice, one must primarily be insightful in the meaning of Hadeeth which is achievable only by acquiring the knowledge of Fiqh. Fiqh ensures the texts are contextualized and practiced properly. Shaykh Al-Awwāmah ﷺ quotes some of the renowned Muhaddithoon and Fuqahā explaining the necessary relationship between Hadeeth and Fiqh. Fiqh serves as a supplementary guide towards understanding and practicing upon Hadeeth;

1. Abu Na'eem relates from Abdur Rahmān Al-Mahdi ﷺ (titled the leader of the Believers in Hadeeth), "No person is worthy of leadership in Hadeeth until he is able to distinguish between authentic and non-authentic reports, inferable and non-inferable reports and know where was the knowledge acquired from."

2. Imām Muzani ﷺ, (a renowned Shāfi'ee scholar) states, "May Allāh ﷺ show mercy on you, ponder over the Ahādeeth which you have collated. If you acquire knowledge from the jurists, then you will be amongst the Fuqahā (jurists)."

3. Imām Mālik ﷺ said, "Practice upon Hadeeth the way the Fuqahā have practiced upon it."

4. Ibn Wahb ﷺ states, "Any person who has knowledge of Hadeeth but no reference to Fiqh is misguided. Had Allāh ﷺ not saved us through Imām Mālik and Layth, then surely we would have strayed (from the true path)."

5. Sufyān Ibn Uyayna ﷺ states, "Hadeeth can become a means of misguidance for people except for the Fuqahā."

6. Rajā Al-Harawi ﷺ states, "Whoever learns Hadeeth without Fiqh is like a pharmacist who amasses medicines without knowing which applies to what, until the physician comes. Thus he remains a student of Hadeeth and does not know the

application of the Hadeeth until a Faqeeh comes." (cited in *The four Imāms and their school, by Gibril Haddād* p. 118)

All of the above statements imply to the fact that Fiqh plays a vital role for explaining Hadeeth in terms of its correct application and the manner it ought to be practiced. Thus, determining the practice of Hadeeth to become necessary solely on the basis of the soundness of the chain of transmitters is inadequate.

Another reason why it is insufficient to consider the practicing upon a Hadeeth as mandatory solely based on the soundness of its chain is that there are instances where two or more authentic reports conflict with one another. One must be acquainted with the science of conflict resolution in Hadeeth, an independent discipline which only the Fuqahā possess.

I cited one example of two rigorously authentic Hadeeths conflicting with each other under the title *Classifications of Texts*. I will present another example below to illustrate this complexity with regards to a simple matter of drinking water, whether one should stand up and drink or sit down?

1.   Sayyidunā Nizāl Ibn Sabura ﷺ once came to the door of Habba and <u>drank whilst standing</u> and he said, "Verily I saw the Messenger of Allāh ﷺ do the way you have seen me do." (Bukhāri)

2.   Sayyidunā Abdullāh Ibn Umar ﷺ relates, "We would eat during the time of the Messenger of Allāh ﷺ whilst walking and <u>we would drink whilst standing."</u> (Tirmizi)

3. Amr Ibn Shuaib relates from his father (Shuaib) who relates from his grandfather (Sayyidunā Abdullāh Ibn Amr Ibnul Ās ﷺ) that, "I saw the Messenger of Allāh ﷺ <u>drinking whilst standing and also sitting.</u>" (Tirmizi)

4. Sayyidunā Anas Ibn Mālik ﷺ relates that the Messenger of Allāh ﷺ <u>forbade that a man drinks whilst standing</u>. Qatādah (a Tābi'ee) states that we enquired from Sayyidunā Anas about eating (whether standing up and eating is permissible)? He replied, "That (eating whilst standing) is *asharr* (far worse) and *akhbath* (immoral)." (Muslim)

5. Sayyidunā Abū Hurairah ﷺ relates that the Messenger of Allāh ﷺ said, "<u>No one amongst you should drink whilst standing. But whoever forgets, then he should vomit.</u>" (Muslim).

All of the above Ahādeeth apparently conflict with one another inspite of the soundness of their chain of transmitters. Hadeeths (1) & (2) permit drinking water whilst standing. Hadeeth (3) permits drinking water whilst standing and sitting. However, Hadeeths (4) & (5) prohibit drinking water whilst standing and Hadeeth (5) goes to the extent of instructing one to vomit because of drinking whilst standing. The complexity involved at this stage is whether reconciliation between the conflicting reports is possible or not, and if so then on what basis will this be done? Or whether in such instance the jurist will leave a side an authentic report in favour of another authentic or an external evidence.

This is a clear illustration that it is insufficient to consider it necessary to act upon on the apparent meaning of Hadeeth based on its rigorous authenticity. In cases such as the one above, one is now compelled to resort to the works of the classical Fuqahā to seek answers. The principle which the Hadeeth scholars employ to resolve contradictory reports have themselves been established by the four Imāms, but differ in their respective method and approach.

When two Hadeeth conflict with each other, the matter becomes ambiguous and opened to more than one interpretation. It is in these matters that Taqleed of a legal jurist is made and not in following any random person. It is made by following religious experts who are also righteous and pious. The fact that the vast majority of the Ummah in the past adhered to one of the four schools and the statements of some (amongst many) distinguishing scholars about following a particular school, establishes the need for the Ummah to adhere to one of the four schools of today.

A final point to mention is the question of infallibility. Undoubtedly, the four Imāms are fallible in comparison to the Messenger of Allāh ﷺ. However, considering their level of scholarship and expertise and the fact that thousands of scholars throughout centuries adhered to one of the four schools and adopted their interpretive model of the Sharī'ah, does that not make them infallible in comparison to today's individuals or minority advocates of the abandonment of Taqleed? What guarantee can such advocates give that their method of interpretation of the Qur'ān and Sunnah and its application is more robust and rigorous compared to the four schools? Such advocates paint a false contrast between the Messenger of Allāh ﷺ and the four Imāms as there is no comparison to be made in the first place. The actual contrast is made between the adherents and non-adherents of a Madhab.

In this way, one shall find that adhering to one of the four schools makes ones practice of religion easy and much more systematic. Apparent contradictions between reports become resolvable by simply following their respective Imām's principles and legal interpretation. On the other hand, abandoning the four Madhabs and then attempting to formulate another legal framework of interpreting the Shar'ee sources is like re-inventing the wheel, a process that requires decades of commitment and even worse, opens an influx of more Madhabs and diverse opinions.

12.2. Is it possible to follow all four schools simultaneously?

Another view that is propagated by some is, why not follow all four schools simultaneously by selecting the soundest opinion? This argument is based on the verse in the Qur'ān, "**Ask the people of remembrance if you do not know" (21:7)**, which permits following the scholars in general, hence does not restrict one to follow one Imām. They then argue that if the view of all four scholars are accepted by the majority of the Ummah and it is accepted that all four are on the truth, then why restrict to one Imām only?

Undeniably we regard all four schools to be on the truth, based on their research methodology of inferring rulings from the Shar'ee sources. However, if a layman under this pretext, begins selecting views randomly from here and there, then the question posed to him is, on what basis has he chosen to act upon the view of this particular Imām in this matter only? He has not reached to the status of Ijtihād nor is he equipped with the science of Hadeeth. Far from being an authority in Hadeeth, he is ignorant of the principles of grading system in Hadeeth. It thus follows, that being selective between Imāms without sound knowledge will ultimately lead towards acting upon whatever conforms to his desires.

Shāh Waliullāh Ad-Dehlawi 🌸, a renowned scholar of Hadeeth, states, "Had the restriction of following only one Imām not existed, then every person would pick and choose those rulings that conformed to his likings. The Deen would become a toy. There is just one solution to this self-conceited problem, which is to restrict the desires by following an expert of Islamic law. This is what Taqleed Shakhsi is about."

12.3. The Statement of Imām Abū Haneefah 🌸, "When a Hadeeth is authentic then that is my Madhab", suggests preferring Hadeeth over the opinion of the Imām.

The above statement apparently suggest to prefer Hadeeth over the statement of the Imām at all times. Hence, if the fatwa of an Imām conflicts with an authentic Hadeeth then simply cast his fatwa aside and practice upon the apparent meaning of the Hadeeth.

Nevertheless, two things have already been made clear from our previous discussion; firstly, the one who has attained the status of Ijtihād and is deeply rooted in the science of Hadeeth can determine whether a Hadeeth is suitable for practice or not. Secondly, it is not always possible to strictly follow authentic Hadeeth because at times, there are other authentic Ahādeeth that will simultaneously contradict it, or the Hadeeth may not be suitable for practice due to certain reasons.

The above statement has been attributed to Imām Abū Haneefah ﷺ as well as to other Imāms also. But unfortunately, it is frequently quoted in a decontextualized manner and reiterated by the non-advocates of Taqleed.

Remember that when Imām Sāhib ﷺ issued this statement, he was not addressing the general public or the laypeople. He was specifically addressing the Mujtahids and scholars rooted in the science of Hadeeth and Fiqh. He was actually attesting to the fact that his research and legal framework was in full conformity with the principles of the Qur'ān and Sunnah. His conclusion and findings were actually based on sound evidences. So framing his statement in another way, it is as though he is stating, "In my Madhab, you shall find authentic Hadeeth." It also implies that if a Hadeeth is later discovered and fulfils the criteria for its soundness and practice according to myself, then include that as part of my Madhab also.

Allāmah Ibn Ābideen Ash-Shāmi ﷺ after quoting the above statement of Imām Sāhib ﷺ comments, "It is no hidden matter that this (expression) is directed at those who are qualified to analyze the texts and recognise the applicable laws from the abrogated ones. When the scholar of the Madhab analyzes the evidence and acts upon it, it will be correct to attribute that (practice) to the Madhab due to the permission granted by the Imām."

(Raddul-Muhtār, vol 1 p.167)

Ibn Katheer 🌸 attributes the above statement to Imām Shāfi'ee 🌸. After discussing the various opinions of the Imāms regarding the meaning of *Salātul Wustā*, he comments on Imām Shāfi'ee's 🌸 statement, "It is a sign of his mastery and trustworthiness, which was also the way of his brother Imāms, may Allāh have mercy on them and be pleased with them." (*Tafseer Ibn Katheer, vol 1 p.654*)

In explaining the above statement, Imām Nawāwi's 🌸 (a renowned Shāfi'ee scholar) further adds the condition of researching the Madhab of the school before preferring Hadeeth over the statement of the Imām. He mentions, "What Imām Shāfi'ee 🌸 said (*when a Hadeeth is authentic then that is my Madhab*) does not mean that anyone who finds a Hadeeth should say, 'This is the Madhab of Imām Shāfi'ee 🌸,' applying the apparent meaning of his statement. What he said most certainly applies to those ranked to the status of Ijtihād in the Madhab. It is a condition for the person to be firmly convinced that either Imām Shāfi'ee 🌸 (or any other Imām in this respect) was unaware of the existence of the Hadeeth or its authenticity. This is only possible after having researched all the books of Imām Shāfi'ee 🌸 and other similar books of the his companions who took knowledge from him and others similar to them." (*Al-Majmu Sharh al-Muhadhab vol 1 p.64*)

Imām Abū Haneefah 🌸 not acting upon a Hadeeth does not always suggest that the Hadeeth did not reach him. Considering the fact that Imām Sāhib 🌸 would only reach to a conclusion after indepth and extensive study of the information and reports transmitted to him, it is possible that Imām Sāhib 🌸 did not act upon a

Hadeeth either because the Hadeeth was not sound according to him, it was abrogated, restricted to a particular instance or it was muqayyad (qualified).

This can be illustrated with two examples;

1. Imām Awza'i ﷺ once approached Imām Sāhib ﷺ during Hajj objecting as to why he discarded the practice of *Raf'ul Yadain* (raising the hands apart from the initial Takbeer on other occasions during Salāh e.g. before and after Ruku)? Imām Awza'i ﷺ narrated the Hadeeth of *Raf'ul Yadain* with his own chain of transmission. Imām Sāhib ﷺ then narrated his Hadeeth of the non-practicing of *Raf'ul Yadain*, not only with his own chain of transmission but also established his chain to be more superior that Imām Awza'i's ﷺ chain of transmission. (*I'lā us Sunan vol 3 p.75*)

2. Imām Abū Yūsuf ﷺ, a prominent student of Imām Sāhib ﷺ as well as a Mujtahid in his own right, states, "I have not seen anyone with insightful knowledge of the meaning of Hadeeth and its application in jurisprudence than Imām Abū Haneefah." He further adds, "Whenever I opposed him and then contemplated over the matter, I would see his position which he adopted to be the most redeeming position in the Hereafter. Whenever I was inclined towards Hadeeth, he would have a deeper insight with the authenticity of Hadeeth than me."

To determine a Hadeeth to be suitable for practice is part of the process of Ijtihād, which requires thorough background research and critical analysis of the textual report as well as the transmitters in the chain. A scholar will strive to act upon what he deems closer to the truth. Each scholar will determine the status of a Hadeeth based on his own criteria, resulting in differences of opinion in the suitability of a Hadeeth; one might consider a Hadeeth to be suitable for practice whilst another may not.

To give an example of differences in criteria, Imām Abū Haneefah ۩ only accepted if the narrator of a Hadeeth transmitted that Hadeeth in the exact verbatim way he heard it from his teacher. He is not permitted to make any additions to the wordings of the Hadeeth. His argument was that making additions to the original text of the Hadeeth will inevitably alter the meaning of the words of the Messenger of Allāh ۩, hence preservation of the original text will not be fulfilled. Other scholars permitted to make minor additions of wordings to the original texts but only under strict conditions.

Another example of differences in criteria is that according to Imām Bukhāri ۩, it is a condition for the person narrating a Hadeeth from his teacher to have remained in his company even momentarily. If he transmits a Hadeeth without remaining in his company then his narration will not be accepted. On the other hand, according to Imām Muslim ۩, his narration is still accepted even if he did not remain in the company of his teacher as long as he lived and heard it directly from the one transmitting it to him.

In summary, Imām Sāhib's ۩ statement as well as the similar statements made by other Imāms, are addressed to the Mujtahid scholars, not to laypersons. Determining a Hadeeth to be authentic and its applicability can only be done by a person with profound understanding of the science of the grading system in Hadeeth and Fiqh. It is only the Mujtahid of the school who decides when to prefer Hadeeth over the statement of the Imām.

12.4. Imām Abū Haneefah's ﷺ knowledge in Hadeeth was weak.

This is a severe allegation made against Imām Abū Haneefah ﷺ. The reason for such an allegation directed against him is because Imām Sāhib ﷺ has not collated any Hadeeth in a book form. Let it be clear that not compiling Hadeeth or transmitting it does not equate to deficiency in the knowledge of Hadeeth. A scholar cannot become a Mujtahid without retaining or memorising Ahādeeth in its abundance nor be insightful in the science of Hadeeth.

Below are testimonies given by scholars of great calibre to Imām Sāhib's ﷺ credibility and his lofty status in Hadeeth;

1. Imām Yahya Ibn Saeed Al-Qattan ﷺ stated: "We have never heard a better understanding of the Qur'ān and Sunnah than that of Abū Haneefah, and we follow him in most of his opinions." (*Al-Bidāyah wan-Nihāyah*, p.418 vol.13)
2. Imām Ad-Dhahabi ﷺ comments about Imām Sāhib ﷺ; "The Imām, the Faqeeh of the nation, the scholar of 'Iraq: Abū Haneefah…," (*Siyar a'lām un-Nubalā*, vol.6 p.390)
3. Imām Yahya Ibn Maeen ﷺ states "Abū Haneefah was a trustworthy narrator. He would only transmit Hadeeth that he had memorised. He would never narrate those Ahādeeth which he had not memorised," (*Tahzeebul-Kamāl*, vol.29,

p.424)

4. Abdullāh Ibnul-Mubārak ﷺ said: "I have not seen a person like him when it comes to comprehending the Deen."

5. Abdullāh Ibnul-Mubārak ﷺ is reported to have said, "If Allāh ﷻ had not benefitted me through Abū Haneefah and Sufyān At-Thawri then I would have been just like an ordinary person." (*Tabyeed As-Shifā* p.16-17)

6. Muhammad Ibn Sama'ā ﷺ states, "The Imām has mentioned more than seventy thousand Ahādeeth in his book and has selected Āthār (reports) from forty thousand Ahādeeth." (*I'lā us-Sunan*, vol 19 p.315)

7. Shāh Waliullah Ad-Dehlawi ﷺ asserts the Madhab of Imām Abū Haneefah ﷺ to be based on sound Ahādeeth and reports. He states, "Undoubtedly, the Madhab of the Imām is based upon sound Ahādeeth and strong reports. What he has mentioned in our books (of jurisprudence) are with rational evidences and juristic analogy, that is specifically (employed) to prefer some Ahādeeth over the other (through rational evidences)." (*Muqaddamatul-Lam'āt*, vol 1 p.18)

13. Conclusion

Our discussion has by now made it clear that Taqleed is not a new phenomenon. Its existence has been since the early Muslim generation. Taqleed is about relying and following experts in Islamic Law, namely legal jurists or Mujtahids. The process of Taqleed underwent some serious evolvement from Ām (general) to Shakhsi (individual school). Taqleed of one of the four Madhabs became necessary due to the following reasons;

1. None of the other Madhabs gained recognition and acceptance as the four major Madhabs did.
2. The robustness of the four Madhabs enabled them to solve unprecedented legal issues in every generation.
3. Their juristic principles, detailed Fiqhi cases and elaboration on legal texts were codified, refined and developed by their reputable students and by the end of the fourth era, only their principles served as an accepted interpretive model for the Shari'ah.
4. Many reputable scholars of the past adhered to one of the four legal schools, each one being an expert in his own right.
5. A layperson, being oblivious of the science of Hadeeth and juristic principles, is unable to distinguish between suitable and non-suitable practices of Hadeeth.
6. Following one of the four Madhabs will be a means of controlling ones egos and desires. The Deen will become much more systematic and easier to follow.
7. Abandoning the four legal schools will result in creating a fifth Madhab and opening a floodgate of more diverse opinions and confusion on single matters.

PART TWO:

Common Questions on Taqleed

What Does Taqleed Mean?

Q What is the definition of Taqleed? Will a person still remain a Hanafi if he acts upon Imām Abū Yūsuf's ⬧ or Imām Zufar's ⬧ view? Also will he still remain a Hanafi if he acts upon the opinion of Imām Shāfi'ee ⬧ or Imām Mālik ⬧ at the time of need?

A Definition: Taqleed means, to follow and accept the opinion or a legal verdict of a particular Mujtahid, without demanding evidence from him. The Mujtahid must have attained the highest calibre and proficiency in the four sources of Islamic Law i.e. the Holy Qur'ān, Hadeeth, Ijmā and Qiyās, and mastered all of the necessary requirements, in order to achieve that status of proficiency, along with meeting the spiritual requirements. This is known as Taqleed.

The statement 'without demanding proof', does not imply that it is impermissible to demand proof, nor does it imply that the Imām will have no evidence at all. Rather, it suggests accepting the Imām's statement, with the conviction that his legal opinion has been derived from the four sources of Shari'ah i.e. the Holy Qur'ān, Hadeeth, Ijmā and Qiyās. Therefore, there is no need to ask for any proof, due to his expertise. For a non-Mujtahid to follow a Mujtahid, trusting that he has the proof and evidence, without asking him for the evidence, is also known as Taqleed.

It is the jurisprudential principles set by Imām Abū Haneefah ⬧, that his students, such as Imām Abū Yūsuf ⬧ and others, have used and developed through the course of time, in order to derive further Masā'il related to Shari'ah. Whether these Masā'il are directly from Imām Sāhib ﷺ or not, a person who follows them will still remain a 'Hanafi'.

The views of Imām Sāhib's ﷺ students are in actual fact, Imām Sahib's ﷺ views. Therefore, not acting upon Imām Sāhib's ﷺ opinion and preferring his student's opinion, on specific occasions, does not expel an individual from the Hanafi Madhab. Rather, he will remain a Hanafi. (Rasmul Mufti by Allāmah Shāmi ﷺ).

Furthermore, due to the change of time, customs and occurrences, a ruling of one issue can vary. However, the scholars of the latter era understood that if Imām Sāhib ﷺ was alive today, he would have also issued a similar verdict. Therefore, they would issue a different ruling, regardless of whether that was the same view of Imām Shāfi'ee ﷺ or of any other Imām.

Should we Follow a Particular Madhab in Matters of Shari'ah Law?

Q Some people assert that Taqleed (following the school of an Imām) is unlawful in Shari'ah. They insist that a true Muslim should directly follow the Holy Qur'ān and Sunnah and following a Madhab of an Imām, in the matters of Shari'ah, is equivalent to Shirk (polytheism). They also claim that the Hanafi, Shāfi'ee, Māliki and Hanbali schools were formed some two hundred years after the departure of the Holy Prophet ﷺ from this world; therefore, these schools are an innovation (Bid'ah). Some also stress, that a Muslim should seek guidance directly from the Holy Qur'ān and Sunnah and no intervention of an Imām is needed to practice upon the Shari'ah. Please explain how far this view is correct.

A Shaykh Mufti Taqi Uthmāni Sāhib has given the following response in regards to this assertion: This view is based on certain misunderstandings arising from unnecessary treatment of the complicated issues involved. The full clarification of this mistaken view requires a detailed article. However, I will try to explain the basic points as briefly as possible.

It is true that obedience, in its true sense, belongs to Allāh ﷻ alone. The obedience of the Holy Prophet ﷺ, has also been ordained upon us, because he conveyed to us the divine commandments of Allāh ﷻ; otherwise he has no status deserving our obedience. By obeying and acting according to the teachings of the Holy Prophet ﷺ, we obtain the pleasure of Allāh ﷻ.

72

However, the root of the matter is, that the interpretation of the Holy Qur'ān and Sunnah is not a simple one. It requires an intensive and extensive study of the sacred sources of Shari'ah, which cannot be undertaken by a person unqualified in the field. If every Muslim was obliged to directly resort to the Holy Qur'ān and Sunnah on each and every problem arising before him, it would burden him with a responsibility that would be almost impossible to fulfil. This is because the derivation of the rules of Shari'ah from the Holy Qur'ān and Sunnah, requires a thorough knowledge of the Arabic language and all the relevant sciences - a combination which every person is not known to have. The only solution to this problem is that, a few individuals from each locality should undertake the responsibility of acquiring an in depth knowledge of the Islamic Law, so that other members in that locality could enquire from them, the ruling of an issue occurring in their day-to-day affairs. This is exactly what Allāh ﷻ has ordained for the Muslims in the following words:

"And not (all of) the Believers should advance altogether, so from every group why shouldn't there be a party that would go forth, that they (who are left behind) may attain (a deep) understanding in religion, so that they may warn their people when they return to them, so that they may beware (of evil)." (9:122).

This verse of the Holy Qur'ān indicates in clear terms, that a group of Muslims should devote themselves to acquiring the knowledge of Shari'ah and all others should consult them for the rulings. Now, if a person asks a reliable scholar about the juridical (Shari'ah) ruling regarding a specific matter and acts upon his advice, can any reasonable person accuse him of committing Shirk on the ground that he has followed the advice of a human being, instead of the Holy Qur'ān and Sunnah? Certainly not.

The reason is obvious, because he has not abandoned obedience to Allāh ﷻ and His Messenger ﷺ. Rather, he is in search of a way to obey them. Being unaware of the Shari'ah commands, he has consulted a scholar, in order to know what he is required to do by Allāh ﷻ. He has not taken that scholar as the subject of his obedience, but rather, as an interpreter of the divine commands. Nobody can accuse him of committing Shirk.

This is the essence of Taqleed; whereby a person who does not have an in-depth understanding of the legal applications of the Holy Qur'ān and Sunnah, resorts to the interpretation of a Muslim jurist, often termed an Imām, and acts according to his interpretation of the Shari'ah. The person never considers the Imām worthy of obedience, nor binding upon him, but seeks his guidance, in order to know the requirements of the Shari'ah.

Fiqh-ul-Imām - This is due to not having direct access to the Holy Qur'ān and Sunnah or not having adequate knowledge for deriving the rules of Shari'ah from these sources. This behaviour is called Taqleed of that jurist or Imām. Thus, how can it be said that Taqleed is equivalent to Shirk?

The qualified Muslim jurists or Imāms, who have devoted their lives to Ijtihād, have collected the rules of Shari'ah, according to their respective interpretations of its sources, in an almost codified

form. This collection of the rules of Shari'ah, according to the interpretation of a particular jurist, is called the Madhab or "school" of
that jurist.

Thus, the school of an Imām is not something parallel to the
Shari'ah, nor something alien to it. In fact, it is a particular interpretation of the Shari'ah and a collection of the major Shari'ah rules,
derived from the Holy Qur'ān and Sunnah by a reliable jurist and
arranged subject-wise, for the convenience of the followers of the
Shari'ah. So, the one who follows a particular school, actually follows the Holy Qur'ān and Sunnah, according to the interpretation
of a reliable jurist, whom he or she believes to be the most trustworthy and most well-versed in the matters of Shari'ah.

As for the differences in the schools, they have emerged through
the different possible interpretations of the rules, mentioned in or
derived from the Holy Qur'ān and Sunnah. In order to understand
this point properly, it is necessary to know that the rules mentioned in the Holy Qur'ān and Sunnah are of two different categories.

The first category of rules are those which are stated in these sacred sources in such clear words that they allow only one interpretation. No other interpretation is possible thereof, such as the obligation of Salāh, Zakāt, fasting and pilgrimage and the prohibition
of pork and adultery. With regard to this set of rules, no difference
of opinion has ever occurred. All the schools of jurists are unanimous in their interpretation. Hence, there is no room for Ijtihād or
Taqleed in these matters. Also, since everyone can easily under-

stand them from the Holy Qur'ān and Sunnah, there is no need for consulting an Imām or jurist.

On the other hand, there are some rules of Shari'ah derived from the Holy Qur'ān and Sunnah, where any of the following situations may arise:

1) The wording used in the sacred sources may allow more than one interpretation. For example, while mentioning the duration of Iddah (waiting period) for a divorced woman, the Holy Qur'ān has used the following expression, **"And divorced women shall wait (as regards to their marriage) for three periods of Qurū."** (2:228)

The word 'Qurū' used in the above verse has two meanings. It stands both for the 'period of menstruation' and Tuhr (period of cleanliness). Both meanings are possible in the verse and each of them results in different legal consequences.

The question that requires scholarly efforts here is: Which of the two meanings is intended? Whilst answering the question, the juridical opinions may naturally differ, as is the case. Imām Shāfi'ee interprets the word Qurū as the 'period of cleanliness,' while Imām Abū Haneefah interprets it as the 'period of menstruation'. Both of them have a number of reasons in support of their respective views and neither can be completely rejected. This example highlights one of the causes for differences of opinion amongst different schools.

2) Sometimes disparity appears between two Ahādeeth of the Holy

Prophet ﷺ and a jurist has to reconcile between them or prefer one of them over the other. In this case also, the view points of the jurists may differ from one another. For example, there are two sets of traditions found in the books of Ahādeeth, narrating different behaviours of the Holy Prophet ﷺ while performing Rukū in Salāh. The first set of Ahādeeth mention that he used to raise his hands before bowing, while the other Ahādeeth mention that he did not raise his hands except at the beginning of Salāh. The jurists, whilst accepting that both ways are correct, have expressed different views regarding the question: Which of the two ways is more preferable? Thus, situations like these also cause differences of opinion between various schools.

3) There are many issues which are not specifically addressed in the Holy Qur'ān and Sunnah. The solution to these issues is sought either through analogy or through examples, found in the sacred sources, that have an indirect bearing on the subject. Here again, the jurists may have different approaches to extracting the required solution from the Holy Qur'ān and Sunnah.

Such are the basic causes of differences of opinion between the schools. These differences are in no way a defect in Shari'ah; rather, they are a source of flexibility, composing a vast field of academic research, governed by the principles of Shari'ah and settled by means of the Holy Qur'ān and Sunnah, for all time to come.

A Muslim jurist, who has all the necessary qualifications for Ijtihād, is supposed to attempt his utmost to extract the actual meaning of the Qur'ān and Sunnah. If he does this to the best of his ability and with sincerity, he will be rewarded for accomplishing his duty and nobody can accuse him of disregarding the Shari'ah, even though his view may seem to be weaker when compared to others. This is a natural and logical circumstance, certain to be found in every legal system.

The established laws in every legal framework do not cover every minute detail and possible situation. Also, these laws are often open to more than one interpretation. Different courts of law, while attempting to understand them, often disagree about their meanings. One court may interpret the law in a particular way, while another court may understand it in quite a different sense. Thus, nobody can say that the jurists have disrespected the laws of Islām by arriving at different opinions. And since every court of law intends to apply the established law to the best of its ability, its duty towards the Lawmaker (Allāh ﷻ) will be discharged and its jurists will be rewarded for it.

For example, if one of the courts mentioned earlier was a high court, all the lower courts and the people living under its authority would be bound to follow judgements made by the high court, even though their personal opinion might not conform to the opinion of the high court. In such a case, if the lower courts follow the decision of the high court, nobody can say that they are not following the law or that they take the high court to be a legislator of the law. This is because, in actual fact, the lower courts are following the decision of the high court as a trustworthy interpreter of the law and not as a legislator.

In exactly the same way, the school of a Muslim jurist provides nothing more than a reliable interpretation of the Shari'ah. Another qualified jurist may disagree, regarding the interpretation of that jurist. However, neither can he be accused of disregarding the laws of Shari'ah, nor can anyone accuse the followers of a particular school of following something other than the Shari'ah or committing Shirk. The reason for this is that these Muslims are following the school as a trustworthy interpretation of Shari'ah.

The next question which may arise here is: What should a person do with regard to these different schools and which one of them should he follow? The answer to this question is very simple. All of these schools have been sincere in their efforts to infer the true meaning of the Shari'ah; therefore, they are all equally valid. A person should follow the school of any of the recognised Imāms, whom he believes to be most knowledgeable and most pious.

Although the Muslim jurists who have undertaken the exercise of Ijtihād have been many in number, the schools of the four Imāms - Imām Abū Haneefah ﷺ, Imām Mālik ﷺ, Imām Shāfi'ee ﷺ and Imām Ahmad ﷺ, are found to be more comprehensive, well-arranged and well-preserved up to the present day. The Muslim Ummah as a whole have regarded these four Imāms as having the most reliable interpretations of Shari'ah. The four schools are known as the Hanafi, Māliki, Shāfi'ee and Hanbali schools. The rest of the Madhabs (schools) are either not comprehensive enough, in the sense that they do not contain all aspects of Shari'ah, or have not been preserved in a reliable form. For this reason, the majority of the Muslim Ummah belong to one of these four schools. If a person adopts a school of Islamic law as an interpretation of the Shari'ah, his obligation to follow the Shari'ah stands fulfilled.

This is the true picture of the term Taqleed with reference to the jurisprudential schools. I hope this explanation will be sufficient to show that Taqleed has nothing to do with Shirk or ascribing partners to Allāh ﷻ. It is in fact a simple and easy way of following the Shari'ah.

How Are Laws Deduced from the Holy Qur'ān and Sunnah?

Q How are Masā'il (rulings) derived from the Holy Qur'ān and Sunnah? What methods are used if the Mas'alah cannot be clearly understood from the Holy Qur'ān and Ahādeeth? What is the importance of Taqleed (following a Muslim jurist) in the Shari'ah? Why are we limited to the schools of the four Imāms?

A The original source of guidance is the Holy Qur'ān but generally, it is the fundamental principles and Masā'il which are stated in the Holy Qur'ān. It was the duty of the Holy Prophet 銿 to explain in detail these Masā'il.

Allāh 銿 says, **"And We have revealed to you the Reminder (Qur'ān) so you may explain to mankind of what has been revealed to them so that they may contemplate." (16:44)**

The subject of how the Islamic laws are derived from the Shari'ah sources is a vast subject area. It is impossible to discuss every aspect of it due to its complex nature. However, for simplicity a few basic examples are mentioned below.

Example No. 1

It is stated in the Holy Qur'ān, 'Establish Salāh.' How to perform Salāh is not mentioned at all. The method of performing Salāh, the different types, and their respective rulings are all related to us by the Holy Prophet 銿, through Ahādeeth. For instance, we learn from the Ahādeeth only about aspects such as the number of Rak'ats in each Salāh, in which one is only Sūrah Al-Fātihah recited and in which one an additional Sūrah is recited. Furthermore, which are the ones in which Qirāt is recited quietly and in which one is Qirāt recited loudly. It is impossible to ascertain all this information from the Holy Qur'ān only. Support from the Sunnah is required.

Example No. 2

It is stated in the Holy Qur'ān, 'Pay Zakāt.' The Holy Qur'ān has not mentioned anything regarding this.

All the details on how the Zakāt is calculated on silver, gold, goats, cows, camels etc. have been mentioned in the Ahādeeth.

Example No. 3

It is stated in the Holy Qur'ān, **"And pilgrimage to the house is a duty upon mankind for Allāh for those who can." (3:97)**

The details on how Tawāf should be done and how many rounds there are in one Tawāf, the Masā'il of Arafah, Minā, Muzdalifah and Ramee etc. have all been explained by the Holy Prophet ﷺ.

To understand the Holy Qur'ān, it is important to acquire the knowledge of Ahādeeth. It is impossible to understand the Holy Qur'ān whilst neglecting the Ahādeeth. The Ummah has been commanded to derive guidance from the Holy Qur'ān under the explained instructions of the Holy Prophet ﷺ. In this respect, the obedience of the Holy Prophet ﷺ means the obedience of Allāh ﷻ. **"He who obeys the Prophet has indeed obeyed Allāh." (4:80)**

Likewise, it is mentioned in the Ahādeeth, "Perform Salāh in the manner that you have seen me perform." (Bukhāri) The Holy Prophet ﷺ did not say, pray the way you understand from the Holy Qur'ān.

Different Types of Ahādeeth

Those statements that were made verbally by the Holy Prophet ﷺ himself, are called 'Hadeeth-e-Qawli', and what the Holy Prophet ﷺ practically demonstrated are known as 'Hadeeth-e-Fe'li'. Sometimes, certain actions were done in front of the Holy Prophet ﷺ or were brought to his attention but he did not affirm nor reject them, instead he preferred to remain silent. This is taken as their confirmation. This is called 'Taqreer'. These three types of Ahādeeth are a source of guidance for the entire Ummah.

Qiyās (Analogical Deduction)

Qiyās is the application of Illat (legal cause), also referred to as pretext or prime factor, that is found in the Holy Qur'ān, Sunnah or Ijmā (consensus) to a modern day contemporary issue. This is essentially required when the ruling of a particular contemporary issue is not clearly understood, nor is it found categorically in the Qur'ān, Sunnah or Ijmā. Thus, as a last resort, Qiyās will be used in order to determine the ruling of a contemporary matter, by carefully analysing which prime factor from the Qur'ān, Sunnah or Ijmā is similar to the current issue.

There were certain questions that the Holy Prophet ﷺ was asked. He would reply to them and to further facilitate the questioner's understanding he would sometimes give a logical reason by posing a logical question to the questioner knowing that the answer would become apparent to the questioner.

Example: A Sahābi ﷺ once inquired that since Hajj was due upon his mother (who had passed away), would it be sufficient if he was to perform it on her behalf? The Holy Prophet ﷺ replied in the affirmative. Then he posed a (logical) question to the questioner: Suppose if your mother took a loan from somebody and you paid it off (on her behalf), would it be acceptable or not? The Sahabi ﷺ replied that it would be acceptable. The Holy Prophet ﷺ then said that, paying off the loan to Allāh ﷻ is more worthy to be accepted.

(Bukhāri)

In the Shari'ah this is known as Qiyās, Ijtihād, Istinbāt and I'tibār. Teachings of this nature are supported by the Holy Prophet ﷺ. Its conditions and details can be found in the books of Usūl (Principles of Islamic jurisprudence).

The Holy Prophet ﷺ sent Sayyidunā Mu'ādh Ibn Jabal ﷺ as a judge to Yemen. Whilst he was going, the Holy Prophet ﷺ walked alongside him and gave him a lot of counsel until the Holy Prophet ﷺ came to a point to bid him farewell. During the advice, the Holy Prophet ﷺ asked him, "According to which law will you make your judgements?" He replied, "According to the Holy Qur'ān." The Holy Prophet ﷺ then inquired, "What if you do not find it in the Holy Qur'ān?" He answered, "Then according to the Sunnah of Rasūlullāh ﷺ." Then he asked, "What will you do if you do not find it in the Sunnah either?" He replied, "I will do Ijtihād." The Holy Prophet ﷺ expressed great happiness upon this reply, he was

in full support of this decision and he thanked Allāh ﷻ for this se-
lection. (Abū Dāwood)

Ijtihād
When a Mas'alah cannot be clearly found in the Holy Qur'ān and
the Ahādeeth, then a Mujtahid (jurist) will thoroughly analyse
through analogy and evidences to determine its ruling. This is
known as Ijtihād and Qiyās, as understood from the aforementioned. If this is agreed upon unanimously, it is called Ijmā
(consensus). This is why the Ulamā of Usūl (experts in the field of
juristic principles) have written that, Qiyās does not establish the
decree, but it just makes it evident.

A ruling that exists in the Holy Qur'ān or Ahādeeth, but is not
quite apparent for a layman to understand, maybe made apparent
by a Mujtahid having done Qiyās on its analogies or by analysing
evidently, implicitly or by way of necessity. Imām Bukhāri ﷺ has
compiled a specific chapter regarding this.

Taqleed
The following of a Mujtahid becomes compulsory upon whoever
does not have the capability of Ijtihād. This is known as Taqleed.

The greatest benefit of Taqleed is that it enables ones Deen to be
systematic and easy to practice. Moreover, by practising Taqleed,
there is less probability for the desires to intervene in a person's
Deen. If a person is deprived of Taqleed, he will begin to pick and
choose in Deen those things which are in conformity with his desires in contrast to a Muqallid (a person who practices Taqleed),

for whom there is no scope to 'pick and choose'. This is why Sayyidunā Mu'ādh ﷺ was sent as a judge, so that the Masā'il and rulings he derived from the Holy Qur'ān, Ahādeeth and Ijtihād would be implemented. Following the three principles, mentioned by Sayyidunā Mu'ādh ﷺ would in fact mean obeying the Holy Prophet ﷺ.

It has been narrated from Sayyidunā Abū Hurairah ﷺ, that the Holy Prophet ﷺ said, "Whoever obeyed me has indeed obeyed Allāh ﷻ and whoever disobeyed me has indeed disobeyed Allāh ﷻ; whoever obeyed the Ameer (leader) has indeed obeyed me and whoever disobeyed the Ameer has indeed disobeyed me."

(Bukhāri)

The Categories of Masā'il
There are two types of Masā'il. Firstly, those that have been mentioned in the Nas (Holy Qur'ān or Ahādeeth). Secondly, those which have not been mentioned in the Holy Qur'ān or Ahādeeth.

The first category will further divide into two forms; the first form is that the Nas will either have a ruling in the positive or in the negative only. The second form is, that there are two types of Nas regarding the same Mas'alah. In some we find a ruling in the positive and in others in the negative. For example, from some we find out about Āmeen-bil-Jahr (saying Āmeen loudly) and from some we find about Āmeen-bis-Sirr (saying Āmeen softly). Some inform us about Raf'ul-Yadāyn (raising the hands), whilst others tell us about Tark'ur-Raf'ul-Yadāyn (not raising the hands).

There are also another two groups of Masā'il. The first one is when historic evidence or other circumstances indicate that one Nas has preference over the other. The second type is, when it is not known which Nas has been given preference over the other and nor is it known which came first and which came later. In total there are four types of Masā'il.

First

That type of Nas (evidence that is mentioned in the Holy Qur'ān and Hadeeth) which is so clear, that it only renders one interpretation, giving no scope for any other interpretation. No Qiyās or Ijtihād will be done; neither would Taqleed be permissible if it opposes the Nas. Instead the Nas will be acted upon. All of the four Imāms are unanimous in this category because there can be no scope for differences. For instance the fundamental articles of belief, the prohibition of interest and alcohol etc.

Second

Those Masā'il which have two types of Nas and it is also known which came first and which came second. Generally, the first one will be abrogated, while the second one will be applicable. There is no need for Qiyās, Ijtihād or Taqleed in this type either.

For instance Allāh ﷻ states in the Holy Qur'ān, **"And upon those who have the strength (to fast) is Fidya (compensation)." (2:184)** However, in another place, Allāh ﷻ states, **"So those of you that witness the month (of Ramadhān) must fast." (2:185)**

87

In the early days of Islām, when the Ramadhān fasts were newly prescribed, initially a person was given the option to either fast or give Fidyah, irrespective of whether he or she was rich or poor. The former verse indicates towards this option. Subsequently, this concession was Mansūkh (abrogated) by the latter verse. So now, until the Day of Judgement, whoever has the strength to fast in the month of Ramadhān has to fast. The second verse clearly shows this obligation. In this case, both the Mansūkh (abrogated i.e. the former verse) and the Nāsikh (abrogating i.e. i.e. the latter verse) are known.

Third
Those Masā'il where there are two types of Nas and it is not known which came first and which came second. For instance, the issue of Raf'ul- Yadāyn (raising the hands during Salāh besides the Takbeer-e-Tahreemah) and Tark Raf'ul-Yadāyn (not raising the hands on other occasions besides Takbeer-e-Tahreemah).

Fourth
Those Masā'il regarding which there is no clear Nas at all.

In the last two categories a layman will be in one of two situations; either he is acting upon it or he is not acting upon it and wandering aimlessly. There is no permission for the latter. Allāh 🕮 says, **"Does man think that he will be left in vain?" (75:36).** This is not the case; a person is obliged to obey Allāh's 🕮 commands in every aspect. So which one will he then act upon? In the third category, which Nas does he apply? If he acts upon one, the other is omitted. He cannot prefer one Nas over the other with his own accord because he does not have the knowledge regarding which Nas came first and which came second. Likewise, he will not know which is the abrogator and which is the abrogated. In the fourth category, there is no categorical Nas at all. So without knowledge, what is he going to act upon?

Allāh ﷻ says in the Holy Qur'ān, **"Do not pursue what you have no knowledge about." (17:36)** This leaves no alternative but to do Ijtihād in the third and fourth category. This is because, in the third category one Nas has to be preferred over the other by using other contextual evidences. This must also be done in the fourth category because the ruling has to be found.

It is quite obvious that not everybody has the capability and qualification to do Ijtihād and Istinbāt (deduction of laws). The following verse of the Holy Qur'ān makes this clear; Allāh ﷻ says, **"If they had referred it to the Messenger and to those who have authority amongst them, the proper investigators would have known it from them (direct)." (4:83)**

Anybody can claim to make a decision, regardless of it being right or wrong, but only he will be called a Mustanbit and Mujtahid, who possesses the qualifications of Istinbāt (extensive analysis and deduction) in accordance to the Shari'ah. If he cannot, then he will be known as a Muqallid (follower).

Hence, it is important for a Mujtahid to apply Ijtihād in the third and forth type of Masā'il. As for the Muqallid, it is important for him to do Taqleed. Even if the Mujtahid makes an error, the Mujtahid will not be deprived of reward because his Ijtihād was according to the Shari'ah. If his Ijtihād is correct then he will be entitled to a double reward.

A doubt might arise as to why Taqleed is restricted to the four Imāms (Imām Abū Haneefah ﷺ, Imām Mālik ﷺ, Imām Shāfi'ee ﷺ and Imām Ahmad ﷺ) only, despite there being many Mujtahidoon amongst the Sahābah ﷺ, Tābi'een and Tabi'-Tābi'een? What is the harm in doing Taqleed of anybody else, especially those Sahābah ﷺ whose virtues have been mentioned in the Holy Qur'ān and in many Ahādeeth? The answer to this is that, indeed the Sahābah ﷺ have a higher status than the four Imāms.

The reason for doing Taqleed of the four Imāms in particular, is not because they are thought to be greater than the Sahābah ﷺ. Rather, when doing Taqleed, it is important to acknowledge the Masā'il in which Taqleed is done. There are three fundamental conditions for doing Taqleed of a particular Imām:

a)   That their entire Fiqh and Madhab is preserved from the chapter of purity to inheritance. This is essential so that a person or a scholar can refer to this Imām at all times regarding any aspect of life.

b)   The science of deriving laws and Usūls (jurisprudential principles) have also been preserved, in order for a contemporary scholar to derive new laws on contemporary issues that emerge, based upon the Usūls set by the Imām, that are extracted from the Holy Qur'ān and Sunnah.

c)   The Imām has left behind students and scholars to propagate
      and teach his Fiqh.

Today, there are vast amounts of detail and explanation available
about the Masā'il which have been compiled and collected in the
schools of the four Imāms, from the chapter of Tahārah (purity) to
Kitābul-Farā'idh (chapter on inheritance), including Ibādah, deal-
ings etc. In short, vast numbers of Masā'il, in all the fields and
spheres, have been collected. This type of detailed and compiled
Madhab (school) cannot be found from the Sahābah ﷺ, Tābi'een or
Tabi'-Tābi'een. So, if one was to do Taqleed of anybody apart from
the four Imāms, how would he do it? This is why Taqleed of the
four Imāms alone has been chosen by the scholars.

Allāh ﷻ bestowed upon the four Imāms in-depth knowledge of the
Holy Qur'ān and Ahādeeth and comprehensive skills of Istinbāt
(deduction of laws). They also had access to the Ahādeeth of the
Holy Prophet ﷺ, which were spread throughout the world by the
Sahābah ﷺ.

It is possible that there will be narrations that one Imām knew
about whereas another did not. However, it would be rare to find
narrations that none of them knew about.

Shāh Waliullāh Muhaddith Dehlawi ﷺ has written about the
spreading and circulation of Ahādeeth and about Madeenah being
the headquarters of knowledge. He writes, "These four Imāms are
such that their knowledge collectively encompassed the whole

world and those four Imāms are Imām Abū Haneefah 🐝, Imām Mālik 🐝, Imām Shāfi'ee 🐝 and Imām Ahmad 🐝."

Note: For further clarification on this subject please refer to reliable scholars and authentic books. It must be reminded that this subject is intricate and not easily grasped by a layman. We have merely sufficed on the important aspects of it to illustrate the complexity of this branch of learning.

Why do Taqleed of One Imām only and not Four Simultaneously?

Q Why is it important to do Taqleed of only one Imām? What harm is there in following one Imām for one Mas'alah, then another Imām for another Mas'alah, the way it was in the time of the Sahābah 🙵 and the Tābi'een? They were not dependant on one individual in following the whole Madhab (school of thought).

A During the era of the Sahābah 🙵, virtue and prosperity had the upper hand and generally there was no part in Deen for fulfilling personal desires. That is why when someone inquired about a Mas'alah, he asked with a good intention and acted upon it as well, regardless of whether it coincided with his desires or not.

In later times, this was not the case. Instead, people started having the urge to ask one Mas'alah from a certain Ālim (scholar) and if the answer was against their desires, they would walk off to another Ālim in search of ease. Still not content with this, it became a growing concern about how they would find a way out in every Mas'alah, which would satisfy them. It is apparent that this cannot be the motive for the search of truth.

Sometimes this can cause a lot of damage to a person's Imān. To give an example scenario, if a person made Wudhu and then touched his wife, then somebody following the Madhab (school of thought) of Imām Shāfi'ee 🙵 says to him, "Repeat your Wudhu because touching your wife breaks your Wudhu." He then replies, "I do Taqleed of Imām Abū Haneefah 🙵 and Wudhu does not break in his opinion, in this situation." Then this person vomits. So somebody following the Madhab of Imām Abū Haneefah ﷺ says to him, "Repeat your Wudhu because vomiting breaks the Wudhu, in the opinion of Imām Abū Haneefah ﷺ." He then replies, "I am following the Madhab of Imām Shāfi'ee ﷺ and in his view, Wudhu does not break by vomiting." Now, this person's Salāh is not valid in accordance with the Madhab of Imām Abū Haneefah ﷺ or or that of Imām Shāfi'ee ﷺ. This is known as Talfeeq, which is not permissible by the unanimous decision of the scholars. Following in this manner is in actual fact, not doing Taqleed of any of the Imāms. Rather he is fulfilling his personal desires by picking and choosing which is forbidden in the Shari'ah. It eventually leads a person astray from the path of Allāh ﷻ. Allāh ﷻ says in the Holy Qur'ān, **"And do not follow your personal desires, for they will lead you astray from the path of Allāh." (38:26)**

This is why it is important to do Taqleed of only one particular Imām. The Holy Qur'ān has associated obedience with repentance, **"And follow the path of him who turns to Me." (31:15)**

On this basis, any individual who had a strong presumption about Imām Abū Haneefah ﷺ, that he was repentant and correct and that his Ijtihād was in accordance with the Holy Qur'ān and Ahādeeth, chose to do his Taqleed. Anybody who had the same thought regarding Imām Shāfi'ee ﷺ, Imām Mālik ﷺ or Imām Ahmad ﷺ began doing their Taqleed. Now, it is incorrect to leave ones own Imām whenever a person desires and start following a different Imām. Because without the permission of the Shari'ah it becomes Talfeeq and fulfilment of personal desires which ultimately leads a person astray.

Hence, Shaykh Muhammad Husain Sāhib ﷺ has written in his compilation Ishā'atus-Sunnah, after opposing Taqleed for a very long period of time and then becoming affected with a bitter experience for not doing Taqleed, "We discovered after 25 years of experience that those people who abstain from the Mujtahids and Taqleed eventually bid Islām farewell. Some leave Islām while others end up without any Madhab at all. Rebellion and disobedience of the Shari'ah is a grave result of this freedom."

This is why those learned scholars that had a deep insight of the Holy Qur'ān and countless treasures of the Ahādeeth of the Holy Prophet ﷺ and the Sahābah ﷺ, whose hearts were enriched with fear of Allāh ﷺ and whose lives were enlightened with the light of Sunnah of the Holy Prophet ﷺ, still chose to adopt Taqleed despite having these qualities and virtues within themselves. Moreover, it is also well known that the profound scholars of the six prominent Hadeeth collections i.e. Imām Bukhāri ﷺ, Imām Muslim ﷺ, Imām Tirmizi ﷺ etc, also practiced Taqleed. For example, Imām Abū Dāwood ﷺ was a Hanbali and according to some a Shāfi'ee whilst Imām Muslim ﷺ, Imām Nasai ﷺ, Imām Tirmizi ﷺ and Imām Ibn Mājah ﷺ followed the Shāfi'ee school of thought.

Regarding Imām Bukhāri ﷺ, there are different opinions; according to some he was a Mujtahid whilst other scholars class him to be a Shāfi'ee follower. With the exemption of Imām Bukhāri ﷺ all of the scholars are unanimous that the aforementioned five Muhaddithoon (scholars of Hadeeth) would adhere to a particular Imām.

Moreover, besides the above mentioned eminent Muhaddithoon, there were many other prominent scholars in the past who adhered to a particular Imām. These are as follows:

1. From Amongst the Hanafi School of Thought:

a) Imām Yaqūb Ibn Ibrāheem, famously known as Imām Abū Yūsuf ﷺ, a renowned Faqeeh (jurist), a scholar of Hadeeth and a senior student of Imām Abū Haneefah ﷺ. He was granted the title "Qādhi-ul-Qudhāt" (The judge of judges). Demise 182 A.H.

b) Imām Muhammad Ibn Hasan Ash-Shaybāni ﷺ, also a renowned Faqeeh and a senior student of Imām Abū Haneefah ﷺ. Demise 189 A.H.

c) Muhammad Ibn Abdullāh Al-Muthannah ﷺ, who was from the progeny of a noble Sahābi Sayyidunā Anas Ibn Mālik ﷺ. He was a Qādhi (judge) and amongst the teachers of Imām Bukhāri ﷺ, Imām Ahmad Ibn Hanbal ﷺ and others. Demise 215 A.H.

d) Imām Ahmad Ibn Muhammad Abū Ja'far At-Tahāwi ﷺ. An authority in the field of Hadeeth and also a Faqeeh. He is the author of the Hadeeth collection Sharhul Ma'āni al-Āthār. Demise 321 A.H.

e) Mahmood Ibn Ahmad Al-Badr Al-Ainee ﷺ, famously known as Allāmah Ainee ﷺ, a Muhaddith (an expert in Hadeeth) and the author of Umdatul Qāri which is a volumnous commentary of Saheeh Al-Bukhāri. Demise 855 A.H.

f) Ali Ibn Sultān Muhammad Al-Qāri Al-Harawi, famously known as Mulla Ali Qāri 🌸, a great Muhaddith and the author of Mirqātul Mafātih which is a famous commentary of Mishkātul Masābih. Demise 1014 A.H.

2. From Amongst the Māliki School of Thought:

a) Muhammad Ibn Abdus-Salām, Ibn Suhnūn, Abū Abdullāh Al-Qairawāni 🌸, a very high ranking scholar of Hadeeth. Demise 256 A.H.

b) Hāfiz Ibn Abdul Barr 🌸, a great scholar of Hadeeth. Demise 463 A.H.

c) Ismāeel Ibn Ishāq Abū Ishāq, Al-Qādhi Al-Judhāmi 🌸. Demise 282 A.H.

d) Aslam Ibn Abdul Azeez Ibn Hishām 🌸, Chief Justice of Andalusia and also an expert in Hadeeth. Demise 319 A.H.

3. From Amongst the Shāfi'ee School of Thought:

a) Abū Bakr, Ahmad Ibnul-Husain 🌸 famously known as Imām Baihaqi 🌸, the author of the volumnous Sunan Al-Baihaqi. Demise 458 A.H.

b) Abdullāh Ibn Muhammad, known as Abū Bakr Ibn Abi Shaibah 🌸, a famous teacher of Imām Bukhāri 🌸, Muslim 🌸, Abū Dāwood 🌸 and Ibn Mājah 🌸. Demise 235 A.H.

c) Ahmad Ibn Ali, known as Hāfiz Ibn Hajar Al-Asqalāni 🌸, the author of Fathul Bāri a famous commentary of Saheeh Al-Bukhāri. Demise 852 A.H.

d) Ismāeel Ibn Umar Imād-ud-Deen famously known as Ibn Katheer 🌸, an authority in the field of Tafseer, Hadeeth and Islamic History. He is the author of Tafseer Ibn Katheer (commentary of the Holy Qur'ān), Al-Bidāya Wan-Nihāya (a volumnous collection of Islamic History) and many more. Demise 774 A.H.

e) Muhi-ud-Deen Abū Zakariyyā, Yahyā Ibn Sharaf An-Nawāwi, famously known as Imām Nawāwi 🌸, a profound scholar in Hadeeth and a famous commentator of Saheeh Muslim. Demise 676 A.H.

f) Imām Tabarāni 🌸, the author of Tabarāni. Demise 360 A.H.

4. Followers of the Hanbali School of Thought:

a) Ahmad Ibn Abdul Haleem, known as Abul Abbās Ibn Taimiyah 🌸, an expert in Hadeeth. Demise 728 A.H.

b) Hāfiz Ibn Qayyim Al-Jawziyah 🌸, an expert in various fields and an author of many books. Demise 751 A.H.

c) Abdur Rahmān Ibn Ahmad, known as Ibn Rajab ﷺ, one of the commentators of Saheeh Al-Bukhāri and also Sunan Tirmizi. Demise 795 A.H.

d) Ahmad Ibn Ja'far ﷺ, a teacher of many famous Muhaddithoon such as Dārul Qutni ﷺ and others. Also one of the narrators of Musnad Ahmad. Demise 368 A.H.

The above mentioned eminent scholars are just a few; there are countless scholars up to this day that adhere to one of the Imāms. As we have cited above, it is apparent that it would not be an exaggeration if it was said that these Ulamā reached such a status only through following the Holy Prophet ﷺ and doing Taqleed of the pious servants of Deen and the great Mujtahidoon.

Shaykh Sarfrāz Sāhib ﷺ states, "O readers! This is an ocean that has no shore. Take a look into the books of biographies, the books on the categories of Muhaddithoon, the Fuqahā, the Historians, the Mufassiroon (the commentators of the Holy Qur'ān) and the grammarians and observe. You will certainly find that at least 98% of all of them were Muqallidoon i.e. followed an Imām.

Q If all four Madhabs were in accordance to the Holy Prophet's ﷺ way, then can I follow all four at once?

A Even though all the four Madhabs (schools of thought) are principally correct, in extracting their verdicts from the Holy Qur'ān and Sunnah, the juristic scholars have declared it impermissible for a layman to follow all of the four Madhabs at once. Shaykh Yūsuf Ludhyānwi 🌼 explains this point in detail in his book "Differences in the Ummah and the Straight Path". In summary, it is necessary for a layman who does not possess the qualifications of a Mujtahid to restrict himself to one Madhab only. If a person switches from one Madhab to another, with the claim that all Madhabs are correct that he follows the Holy Qur'ān and Hadeeth, then in spite of making this assertion, he will be following his own understanding and desires.

A layman is in no position to jump to conclusions and to claim what is correct and what is not, if he does not possess the basic qualifications of Ijtihād. If in the worldly affairs, no layman can draw any conclusions on a particular subject without any qualifications then how can such a person draw conclusions about religious matters?

He cannot choose to follow whosoever he wishes in a particular issue. For certain, I can say that, rather than this person adhering to the Deen in the right perspective, he in reality will be following his own desires and do what suits him best under the slogan of 'all the Imāms are correct'. Self-conceit and following ones desires are destructive for ones Deen.

Shaykh Ashraf Ali Thānwi 🌼 states, that a person who follows one Madhab, will have a Deen that is systematic and all his religious obligations will be easier to discharge; whereas a person picking and choosing from one Madhab to another, will have a Deen that is not systematic. If a person was to select all of the strictest rules from all of the Madhāhib, then he will be putting himself into unnecessary difficulty which is wrong. On the other hand, if someone selects all of the easy rulings from all of the Madhāhib, then this becomes personal interest which is also destructive. Hence, to adhere to one Imām will be systematic and free from self-interest. All of the Madhabs in their juristic verdicts and opinions are neither too strict, nor too lenient, but very moderate.

(Ashraful-Jawāb pg.161)

Shāh Waliullāh Dehlawi 🌸 states, "If there was no system of restriction to one school of thought, then every person would pick and choose rulings that conformed to their own whims and desires and Deen would become a toy (in the hands of the masses)." Thus, the only solution to suppress self-interest is to adhere to one Madhab. (Ashraful-Jawāb pg.29)

Moreover, if someone claims that all the four Imāms are right and attempts to follow all of them concurrently, then it will be impossible because one may select one issue from one Imām, whereas, the other Imām may disagree. For instance, if someone bled before Salāh, then according to Imām Abū Haneefah 🌸 the Wudhu will break, whereas Imām Shāfi'ee 🌸 gives the verdict that the Wudhu is intact. On the other hand, if a person touches a woman, then according to Imām Abū Haneefah 🌸 the Wudhu is intact, whereas according to Imām Shāfi'ee 🌸, the Wudhu breaks. If someone selects the flexible laws from these two Madhabs, i.e. does not do Wudhu after bleeding or touching a woman and subsequently offers Salāh in this state, then according to both of the Imāms this person's Salāh is invalid. This is just one example; there are hundreds of more examples, where there are two conflicting opinions amongst the Imāms about a particular issue, i.e. one says it is permissible and one says it is impermissible. The question I ask is, how will such a person's Deen be systematic and easy to follow if one does not possess the qualifications to deduce laws from the Holy Qur'ān and Hadeeth, nor restrict to following one Imām?

This concept of adhering to one Imām is known as Taqleed-e-Shakhsi. This was also practiced by some people during the era of the Sahābah ﷺ, where some adhered to the opinion of one Sahābi ﷺ. Here are some examples: Ikrimāh ﷺ narrates, that the people of Madeenah during Hajj once asked Sayyidunā Abdullāh Ibn Abbās ﷺ a ruling of a particular issue. After receiving an answer, they said, "We will not practice upon your ruling and leave the ruling given by Sayyidunā Zaid Ibn Thābit ﷺ." (Bukhāri)

Imām Tāwoos ﷺ relates that I met seventy from amongst the Companions of the Holy Prophet ﷺ who would resort to the opinion of Sayyidunā Abdullāh Ibn Abbās ﷺ whenever they differed in any matter. (Fawāid-fi-Uloomil-Fiqh)

In conclusion, for the safety of ones Deen and to conduct ones obligations easily, it is necessary to follow one Imām and abstain from attempting to follow all four at once as this would involve self-interest and desire which are detrimental for ones Deen.

Your Questions Answered

An outstanding book written by Shaykh Mufti Saiful Islām. A very comprehensive yet simple Fatāwa book and a source of guidance that reaches out to a wider audience i.e. the English speaking Muslims. The reader will benefit from the various answers to questions based on the Laws of Islām relating to the beliefs of Islām, knowledge, Sunnah, pillars of Islām, marriage, divorce and contemporary issues.

UK RRP: £7.50

Hadeeth for Beginners

A concise Hadeeth book with various Ahādeeth that relate to basic Ibādāh and moral etiquettes in Islām accessible to a wider readership. Each Hadeeth has been presented with the Arabic text, its translation and commentary to enlighten the reader, its meaning and application in day-to-day life.

UK RRP: £3.00

Du'a for Beginners

This book contains basic Du'ās which every Muslim should recite on a daily basis. Highly recommended to young children and adults studying at Islamic schools and Madrasahs so that one may cherish the beautiful treasure of supplications of our beloved Prophet ﷺ in ones daily life, which will ultimately bring peace and happiness in both worlds, Inshā-Allāh.

UK RRP: £2.00

How well do you know Islām?

An exciting educational book which contains 300 multiple questions and answers to help you increase your knowledge on Islām! Ideal for the whole family, especially children and adult students to learn new knowledge in an enjoyable way and cherish the treasures of knowledge that you will acquire from this book. A very beneficial tool for educational syllabus.

UK RRP: £3.00

Treasures of the Holy Qur'an

This book entitled "Treasures of the Holy Qur'ān" has been compiled to create a stronger bond between the Holy Qur'ān and the readers. It mentions the different virtues of Sūrahs and verses from the Holy Qur'ān with the hope that the readers will increase their zeal and enthusiasm to recite and inculcate the teachings of the Holy Qur'ān into their daily lives.

UK RRP: £3.00

Other titles from JKN PUBLICATIONS

Marriage - A Complete Solution

Islām regards marriage as a great act of worship. This book has been designed to provide the fundamental teachings and guidelines of all what relates to the marital life in a simplified English language. It encapsulates in a nutshell all the marriage laws mentioned in many of the main reference books in order to facilitate their understanding and implementation.

UK RRP: £5.00

Pearls of Luqmān

This book is a comprehensive commentary of Sūrah Luqmān, written beautifully by Shaykh Mufti Saiful Islām. It offers the reader with an enquiring mind, Abūndance of advice, guidance, counselling and wisdom.

The reader will be enlightened by many wonderful topics and anecdotes mentioned in this book, which will create a greater understanding of the Holy Qur'ān and its wisdom. The book highlights some of the wise sayings and words of advice Luqmān ﷺ gave to his son.

UK RRP: £3.00

Arabic Grammar for Beginners

This book is a study of Arabic Grammar based on the subject of Nahw (Syntax) in a simplified English format. If a student studies this book thoroughly, he/she will develop a very good foundation in this field, Inshā-Allāh. Many books have been written on this subject in various languages such as Arabic, Persian and Urdu. However, in this day and age there is a growing demand for this subject to be available in English .

UK RRP: £3.00

A Gift to My Youngsters

This treasure filled book, is a collection of Islāmic stories, morals and anecdotes from the life of our beloved Prophet ﷺ, his Companions ﷺ and the pious predecessors. The stories and anecdotes are based on moral and ethical values, which the reader will enjoy sharing with their peers, friends, families and loved ones.

"A Gift to My Youngsters" – is a wonderful gift presented to the readers personally, by the author himself, especially with the youngsters in mind. He has carefully selected stories and anecdotes containing beautiful morals, lessons and valuable knowledge and wisdom.

UK RRP: £5.00

Travel Companion

The beauty of this book is that it enables a person on any journey, small or distant or simply at home, to utilise their spare time to read and benefit from an exciting and vast collection of important and interesting Islamic topics and lessons. Written in simple and easy to read text, this book will immensely benefit both the newly interested person in Islām and the inquiring mind of a student expanding upon their existing knowledge. Inspiring reminders from the Holy Qur'ān and the blessed words of our beloved Prophet ﷺ beautifies each topic and will illuminate the heart of the reader. **UK RRP: £5.00**

Pearls of Wisdom

Junaid Baghdādi ﷺ once said, "Allāh ﷻ strengthens through these Islamic stories the hearts of His friends, as proven from the Qur'anic verse,
"And all that We narrate unto you of the stories of the Messengers, so as to strengthen through it your heart." (11:120)
Mālik Ibn Dinār ﷺ stated that such stories are gifts from Paradise. He also emphasised to narrate these stories as much as possible as they are gems and it is possible that an individual might find a truly rare and invaluable gem among them. **UK RRP: £6.00**

Inspirations

This book contains a compilation of selected speeches delivered by Shaykh Mufti Saiful Islām on a variety of topics such as the Holy Qur'ān, Nikāh and eating Halāl. Having previously been compiled in separate booklets, it was decided that the transcripts be gathered together in one book for the benefit of the reader. In addition to this, we have included in this book, further speeches which have not yet been printed.

UK RRP: £6.00

Gift to my Sisters

A thought provoking compilation of very interesting articles including real life stories of pious predecessors, imaginative illustrations, medical advices on intoxicants and rehabilitation and much more. All designed to influence and motivate mothers, sisters, wives and daughters towards an ideal Islamic lifestyle. A lifestyle referred to by our Creator, Allāh ﷻ in the Holy Qur'ān as the means to salvation and ultimate success.

UK RRP: £6.00

Gift to my Brothers

A thought provoking compilation of very interesting articles including real life stories of pious predecessors, imaginative illustrations, medical advices on intoxicants and rehabilitation and much more. All designed to influence and motivate fathers, brothers, husbands and sons towards an ideal Islamic lifestyle. A lifestyle referred to by our Creator, Allāh ﷻ in the Holy Qur'ān as the means to salvation and ultimate success.

UK RRP: £5.00

Heroes of Islām

"In the narratives there is certainly a lesson for people of intelligence (understanding)." (12:111)

A fine blend of Islamic personalities who have been recognised for leaving a lasting mark in the hearts and minds of people.

A distinguishing feature of this book is that the author has selected not only some of the most world and historically famous renowned scholars but also these lesser known and a few who have simply left behind a valuable piece of advice to their nearest and dearest. **UK RRP: £5.00**

Ask a Mufti (3 volumes)

Muslims in every generation have been confronted with different kinds of challenges. Nevertheless, Islām produced such luminary Ulamā who confronted and responded to the challenges of their time.

"Ask A Mufti" is a comprehensive three volume fatwa book, based on the Hanafi School, covering a wide range of topics related to every aspect of human life such as belief, ritual worship, life after death and contemporary legal topics related to purity, commercial transaction, marriage, divorce, food, cosmetic, laws pertaining to women, Islamic medical ethics and much more.

UK RRP: £30.00

Advice for the Students of Knowledge

Allāh ﷻ describes divine knowledge in the Holy Qur'ān as a 'Light'. Amongst the qualities of light are purity and guidance. The Holy Prophet ﷺ has clearly explained this concept in many blessed Ahādeeth and has also taught us many supplications in which we ask for beneficial knowledge.

This book is a golden tool for every sincere student of knowledge wishing to mould his/her character and engrain those correct qualities in order to be worthy of receiving the great gift of Ilm from Allāh ﷻ. **UK RRP: £3.00**